PAKISTAN

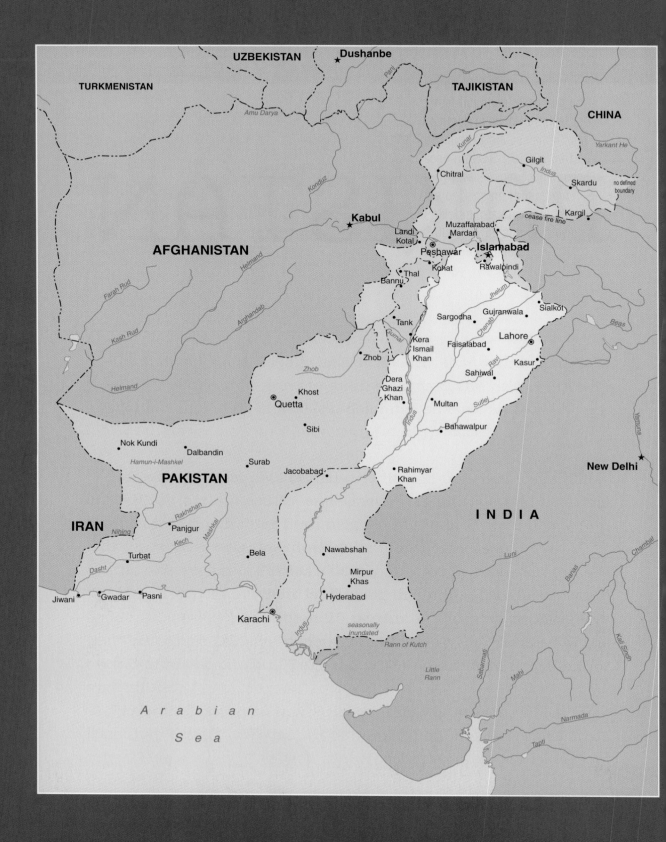

PAKISTAN

Clarissa Aykroyd

MASON CREST
PHILADELPHIA

Mason Crest
450 Parkway Drive, Suite D
Broomall, PA 19008
www.masoncrest.com

©2016 by Mason Crest, an imprint of National Highlights, Inc.

Printed and bound in the United States of America.

CPSIA Compliance Information: Batch #MNMME2016.
For further information, contact Mason Crest at 1-866-MCP-Book.

3 5 7 9 8 6 4 2

Library of Congress Cataloging-in-Publication Data
          on file at the Library of Congress

          978-1-4222-3445-7 (hc)
          978-1-4222-8438-4 (ebook)

Major Nations of the Modern Middle East series ISBN: 978-1-4222-3438-9

TABLE OF CONTENTS

MAJOR NATIONS OF THE MODERN MIDDLE EAST

Afghanistan

Egypt

Iran

Iraq

Israel

Jordan

The Kurds

Lebanon

Pakistan

The Palestinians

Saudi Arabia

Syria

Turkey

KEY ICONS TO LOOK FOR:

 Words to Understand: These words with their easy-to-understand definitions will increase the reader's understanding of the text, while building vocabulary skills.

 Sidebars: This boxed material within the main text allows readers to build knowledge, gain insights, explore possibilities, and broaden their perspectives by weaving together additional information to provide realistic and holistic perspectives.

 Research Projects: Readers are pointed toward areas of further inquiry connected to each chapter. Suggestions are provided for projects that encourage deeper research and analysis.

 Text-Dependent Questions: These questions send the reader back to the text for more careful attention to the evidence presented there.

 Series Glossary of Key Terms: This back-of-the book glossary contains terminology used throughout this series. Words found here increase the reader's ability to read and comprehend higher-level books and articles in this field.

Introduction

by Camille Pecastaing, Ph.D.

O il shocks, wars, terrorism, nuclear proliferation, military and autocratic regimes, ethnic and religious violence, riots and revolutions are the most frequent headlines that draw attention to the Middle East. The region is also identified with Islam, often in unflattering terms. The creed is seen as intolerant and illiberal, oppressive of women and minorities. There are concerns that violence is not only endemic in the region, but also follows migrants overseas. All clichés contain a dose of truth, but that truth needs to be placed in its proper context. The turbulences visited upon the Middle East that grab the headlines are only the symptoms of a deep social phenomenon: the demographic transition. This transition happens once in the life of a society. It is the transition from the agrarian to the industrial age, from rural to urban life, from illiteracy to mass education, all of which supported by massive population growth. It is this transition that fueled the recent development of East Asia, leading to rapid social and economic modernization and to some form of democratization there. It is the same transition that, back in the 19th century, inspired nationalism and socialism in Europe, and that saw the excesses of imperialism, fascism, and Marxist-Leninism. The demographic transition is a period of high risks and great opportunities, and the challenge for the Middle East is to fall on the right side of the sword.

In 1950, the population of the Middle East was about 100 million; it passed 250 million in 1990. Today it exceeds 400 million, to reach about 700 million by 2050. The growth of urbanization is rapid, and concentrated on the coasts and along the few rivers. 1950 Cairo, with an estimated population of 2.5 million, grew into Greater Cairo, a metropolis of about 18 million people. In the same period, Istanbul went from one to 14 million. This expanding populace was bound to test the social system, but regimes were unwilling to take chances with the private sector, reserving for the state a prominent place in the economy. That model failed, population grew faster than the economy, and stress fractures already appeared in the 1970s, with recurrent riots following IMF adjustment programs and the emergence of radical Islamist movements. Against a backdrop of military coups and social unrest, regimes consolidated their rule by subsidizing basic commodities, building up patronage networks (with massive under-employment in a non-productive public sector), and cementing autocratic practices. Decades of continuity in political elites between 1970 and 2010 gave the impression that they had succeeded. The Arab spring shattered that illusion.

The Arab spring exposed a paradox that the Middle East was both one, yet also diverse. Arab unity was apparent in the contagion: societies inspired other societies in a revolutionary wave that engulfed the region yet remained exclusive to it. The rebellious youth was the same; it watched the same footage on al Jazeera and turned to the same online social networks. The claims were the same: less corruption, less police abuse, better standards of living, and off with the tyrants. In some cases, the struggle was one: Syria became a global battlefield, calling young fighters from all around the region to a common cause. But there were differences in the way states fared during the Arab spring. Some escaped unscathed; some got by with a burst of public spending or a sprinkling of democratic reforms, and others yet collapsed into civil wars. The differential resilience of the regimes owes to both the strength and cohesiveness of the repressive apparatus, and the depth of the fiscal cushion they could tap into to buy social peace. Yemen, with a GDP per capita of $4000 and Qatar, at $94,000, are not the same animal. It also became apparent that, despite shared frustrations and a common cause, protesters and insurgents were extremely diverse.

Some embraced free-market capitalism, while others clamored for state welfare to provide immediate improvements to their standards of living. Some thought in terms of country, while other questioned that idea. The day after the Arab spring, everyone looked to democracy for solutions, but few were prepared to invest in the grind of democratic politics. It also quickly became obvious that the competition inherent in democratic life would tear at the social fabric. The few experiments with free elections exposed the formidable polarization between Islamists and non-Islamists. Those modern cleavages paralleled ancient but pregnant divisions. Under the Ottoman Millet system, ethnic and sectarian communities had for centuries coexisted in relative, self-governed segregation. Those communities remained a primary feature of social life, and in a dense, urbanized environment, fractures between Christians and Muslims, Shi'as and Sunnis, Arabs and Berbers, Turks and Kurds were combustible. Autocracy had kept the genie of divisiveness in the bottle. Democracy unleashed it.

This does not mean democracy has to forever elude the region, but that in countries where the state concentrates both political and economic power, elections are a polarizing zero-sum game—even more so when public patronage has to be cut back because of chronic budget deficits. The solution is to bring some distance between the state and the national economy. If all goes well, a growing private sector would absorb the youth, and generate taxes to balance state budgets. For that, the Middle East needs just enough democracy to mitigate endemic corruption, to protect citizens from abuse and extortion, and to allow greater transparency over public finances and over licensing to crony privateers.

Better governance is necessary but no sufficient. The region still needs to figure out a developmental model and find its niche in the global economy. Unfortunately, the timing is not favorable. Mature economies are slow growing, and emerging markets in Asia and Africa are generally more competitive than the Middle East. To succeed, the region has to leverage its assets, starting with its geographic location between Europe, Africa, and Asia. Regional businesses and governments are looking to anchor themselves in south-south relationships. They see the potential clientele of hundreds of millions in Africa and South Asia reaching middle class status, many of whom Muslim. The Middle East can also count on its vast sources of energy, and on the capital accumulated during years of high oil prices. Financial investments in specific sectors, like transport, have already made local companies like Emirates Airlines and DP World global players.

With the exception of Turkey and Israel, the weakness is human capital, which is either unproductive for lack of adequate education, or uncompetitive, because wage expectations in the region are relatively higher than in other emerging economies. The richer Arab countries have worked around the problem by importing low-skilled foreign labor—immigrants who notoriously toil for little pay and even less protection. In parallel, they have made massive investments in higher education, so that the productivity of their native workforce eventually reaches the compensations they expect. For lack of capital, the poorer Arab countries could not follow that route. Faced with low capitalization, sticky wages and high unemployment, they have instead allowed a shadow economy to grow. The arrangement keeps people employed, if at low levels of productivity, and in a manner that brings no tax revenue to the state.

Overall, the commerce of the region with the rest of the world is unhealthy. Oil exporters tend to be one-product economies highly vulnerable to fluctuations in global prices. Labor-rich countries depend too much on remittances from workers in the European Union and the oil-producing countries of the Gulf. Some of the excess labor has found employment in the jihadist sector, a high-risk but up and coming industry which pays decent salaries. For the poorer states of the region, jihadists are the ticket to foreign strategic rent. The Middle East got a taste for it in the early days of the Cold War, when either superpower provided aid to those who declared themselves in their camp. Since then, foreign strategic rent has come in many forms: direct military aid, preferential trade agreements, loan guarantees, financial assistance, or aid programs to cater to refugee populations. Rent never amounts to more than a few percentage points of GDP, but it is often enough to keep entrenched regimes in power. Dysfunction becomes self-perpetuating: pirates and jihadists, famine and refugees, all bear promises of aid to come from concerned distant powers. Reforms lose their urgency.

Turkey and Israel have a head start on the path to modernization and economic maturity, but they are, like the rest of the Middle East, consumed in high stakes politics that hinder their democratic life. Rather than being models that would lift others, they are virtually outliers disconnected from the rest of the region. The clock is ticking for the Middle East. The window of opportunity from the demographic transition will eventually close. Fertility is already dropping, and as the current youth bulge ages it will become a burden on the economy. The outlook for capital is also bleak. Oil is already running out for the smaller producers, all the while global prices are pushed downwards by the exploitation of new sources. The Middle East has a real possibility to break the patterns of the past, but the present is when the transition should occur.

This photo shows a 2010 test firing of a Pakistani Hatf V ballistic missile, which is capable of carrying a nuclear warhead deep into Indian territory. Both Pakistan and its long-time antagonist India are nuclear powers, which has made finding peaceful solutions to Kashmir and other conflicts essential to regional security.

Pakistan's Place in the World

Established as an independent state in 1947, Pakistan is relatively young, although this country in southern Asia contains traces of some of the world's most ancient civilizations. Pakistan means "the land of the pure" in Urdu, the national language. Unfortunately, the creation of the new country resulted in one of the 20th century's most sudden and bloody conflicts.

With its heart-stopping vistas of jagged mountains and forested lowlands, Pakistan has lured the adventurous for thousands of years. The country's trading partners have seen it as a source of important natural resources, and it has also served as a strategic base for broader control of Asia and the Middle East.

In the past, the region that is now Pakistan was dominated by a succession of world powers, and throughout its history the inhabitants were influenced by three major religions—Buddhism, Hinduism, and Islam. Today, the country is unified by Islam, the religion practiced by nearly all its citizens. During the years leading up to the 1947 partition of India, which was then a colony of Great Britain that included modern-day Pakistan, many Indian Muslims longed for their own land where they could practice their religion.

Today, the principles of Islam govern nearly all aspects of life in Pakistan, including festivals, food, clothing, schools, and attitudes toward women. At the same time, this does not mean all Pakistani Muslims worship and act in exactly the same way. Both of Islam's main branches, Sunni and Shia, have strong followings in the country.

The presence of a common religion in Pakistan has not prevented fighting between different tribes and ***ethnic*** groups within the country, however. Pakistan contains several major ethnic groups, who speak a variety of languages. And although the founders of modern Pakistan had high ideals, from the beginning political divisions, corruption, and widespread poverty have dogged the nation. In addition, for 25 years after its formation, the country suffered from a major geographical division—West Pakistan and East Pakistan were separated by 1,000 miles (1,600 kilometers) of Indian territory. This separation made the country very unstable and eventually resulted in East Pakistan declaring independence as Bangladesh in 1971.

Today, instability still accompanies some of Pakistan's foreign relations. The country historically has had close cultural and religious ties with its immediate neighbor, Afghanistan. Pakistan has had to shelter many Afghan refugees of war, and was one of the few

Words to Understand in This Chapter

ethnic—relating to a group of people with a common national, cultural, or racial background.
Sikhs—followers of Sikhism, a religion influenced by both Hinduism and Islam.

nations that recognized the legitimacy of Afghanistan's repressive Taliban government, which ruled the country from 1996 to 2001.

INTERNATIONAL TENSIONS

For more than 60 years, Pakistan has been at odds with its largest neighbor, India, where most of the population is Hindu. Immediately after the partition of India and Pakistan, a war broke out between the two countries in which an estimated 250,000 people were killed. A major refugee crisis also developed, during which large numbers of Hindus and **Sikhs** left Pakistan and moved to India. At the same time, Muslims fled India for Pakistan. Historians estimate that more than 12 million people became refugees immediately after the 1947 partition.

Disputes over certain regions—particularly Jammu and Kashmir, a province of India with a Muslim majority—have been violent and continuous, erupting into full-fledged war in 1965 and again in 1971. The world has viewed the tense relationship between the two countries with great anxiety, and the United States

Armed soldiers patrol the border between India and Pakistan. Both sides claim the region known as Jammu and Kashmir, which is controlled by India although most of the people are Muslims.

and other world powers have involved themselves in peace negotiations. The situation between India and Pakistan has become worse since the mid-1990s, when both countries developed nuclear weapons. A full-scale war between these longtime adversaries now has the potential for millions of deaths and nuclear devastation throughout Central and Southern Asia.

In the years following the September 2001 terrorist attacks in New York and Washington, D.C., Pakistan has assisted the United States in the war against international terrorism. Between September 2001 and September 2004, Pakistani security forces arrested more than 600 people suspected of being members of al Qaeda, the terrorist network believed to have planned the 2001 attacks. The military has also assisted U.S. operations to capture top al Qaeda leaders along the Afghanistan border. As a result, in March 2004 the U.S. State Department elevated Pakistan's status to that of a major non-NATO ally. This upgrade allowed for closer military cooperation between the two countries and permitted Pakistan to buy military supplies and equipment from the United States, which would better enable the military to fight a conventional war against India, should one break out.

However, Pakistan is a sovereign country that has relationships with many countries other than the United States. Subsequently, Pakistan's interests do not always align with the interests of the superpower. In early 2004 U.S. leaders became upset when they learned that the head of Pakistan's nuclear program, Dr. Abdul Qadeer Khan, had shared nuclear secrets with Iran, Libya, and North Korea—all of which were on the U.S. State Department's list of countries that sponsor international terrorism. By 2008, American officials had come to believe that leaders of the Pakistani intelligence agency Inter-Services Intelligence (ISI) were tipping off militants so they could avoid capture by U.S. forces in neighboring Afghanistan. There have been several skirmishes between U.S. and

Pakistani forces on the Pakistan-Afghanistan border, and many Pakistanis were angered by a May 2011 U.S. special forces raid on Abbottabad, where the terrorist leader Osama bin Laden had been hiding in a compound. The U.S. did not notify Pakistan's government about the operation, in which bin Laden was killed, until after it was over. Pakistanis have also been concerned about the U.S. program of drone attacks on suspected terrorists. Thus the relationship between the two nations has remained cool, although the United States still provides more of Pakistan's financial and military aid than any other country.

Despite decades of turmoil in Pakistan, both within its borders and with other countries, the people are determined to face the future with dignity and optimism.

 Text-Dependent Questions

1. What is the predominant religion of Pakistan?
2. What happened to the state of East Pakistan in 1971?

 Research Project

Using the Internet or your school library, research the state of Jammu and Kashmir. What are the major cities in this region? How many people live there? What are the main industries, and how are the people employed? What problems do people face in their everyday lives? Write a two-page report on what life is like in this state, and present it to your class.

Pakistan is home to some of the highest mountains in the world. The mountain pictured here is Nanga Parbat, part of the Himalayan range. It is one of four mountains in Pakistan higher than 26,000 feet.

The Land

Pakistan is located in South Asia and shares borders with four other countries. Iran and Afghanistan sit on the country's western border; China lies to the northeast; and India is located to the east and southeast. Pakistan's largest river, the Indus, enters the country from India and travels southwest until it reaches the Arabian Sea, which runs along Pakistan's southern border.

The country is divided into four provinces: Sindh, Punjab, Balochistan, and Khyber Pakhtunkhwa, called the North-West Frontier Province until 2010. It is slightly less than twice the size of California, covering an area of 307,374 square miles (796,095 sq km).

Extreme climate conditions and geographical features render much of Pakistan uninhabitable, though there are several cities dispersed throughout the country. These centers are attracting increasing numbers of the population's nearly 200 million inhabitants. On the outskirts of the cities and beyond, *rural* village life remains much as it was hundreds of years ago.

Pakistan can be separated into four major geographical areas: the northern mountains, the vast Balochistan plateau in the west, the southeastern desert, and the plains of the Indus River, located in the country's eastern half.

THE NORTHERN MOUNTAINS

The mountainous region of northern Pakistan, where several ranges meet, have some of the world's highest peaks. The Himalayan mountain range, which covers much of the country's northern corner, has four peaks higher than 26,000 feet (8,000 meters). Further north is the Karakoram range, part of the greater Himalayan system, which also runs through Tajikistan, China, Afghanistan, and India. Rising straight up from the valley floors, the mountains of the Karakoram are even more spectacular than those of the southern Himalayas. K2, also known as Mount Godwin-Austen, reaches 26,656 feet (8,611 meters) in height and is the second-highest mountain in the world after Mount Everest. The Hindu Kush range stretches across northwestern Pakistan into Afghanistan. The edges of the Pamir range, mostly located in Tajikistan, also reach into part of northern Pakistan.

Below these mountain ranges, the valleys have relatively little vegetation. Although some of the region is heavily forested, many of

Words to Understand in This Chapter

delta—area where the water from a river is deposited into the sea.
irrigation—method of supplying water to areas of land.
monsoon—a seasonal wind that determines the climate of large regions.
rural—of the countryside.

The Indus River snakes through the sandy floor of the Skardu Valley.

the valleys are dry and desert-like. In the magnificent Skardu Valley, on the edge of the Karakoram, sand dunes line the banks of the Indus River. The small numbers of people who live in the region of the northern mountains cultivate barley and fruit, especially apricots. Because most precipitation only falls high up in the mountains, farmers depend heavily on ***irrigation*** sources.

Many wild animals live in the northern mountains, although some of them are rarely seen. The brown bear, the black Himalayan bear, and various kinds of wild sheep and goats make the mountains their home. The beautiful snow leopard also lives in this region.

THE BALOCHISTAN PLATEAU

Few people live on the Balochistan plateau, although it covers more than a third of Pakistan's total area. With an extreme climate and barren landscape, this plateau has long been considered one of the least inhabitable regions of Pakistan. An Arab poet once wrote of the Balochistan plateau, "Oh Allah, seeing thou hast created Balochistan, / What need was there of conceiving Hell?"

The Sulaiman Mountains cut a forbidding barrier on the northeastern edge of the Balochistan plateau. These mountains extend from Pakistan's northern ranges, though they are not nearly as high. The twin peaks of Takht-e-Sulaiman, at 11,295 feet (3,443 meters) and 11,085 feet (3,379 meters), offer magnificent views over the plateau to the west and south and the Indus River valley to the east. According to legend, Takht-e-Sulaiman (Persian for "throne of Solomon") is where the revered patriarch ordered his flying throne be placed. He was fulfilling a request from his newly wed Indian bride, who wanted to take one last look at her homeland before she left. The mountains are also known for pine trees that produce edible pine nuts.

Did You Know?

The Karakoram mountain range has some of the longest glaciers in the world outside the polar regions. The longest of these formations include the Siachen glacier, which extends 46 miles (74 km), and the Batura glacier, which extends 41 miles (65 km).

The Kirthar Range marks the southeastern edge of Balochistan. The range, whose mountains are shorter than the Sulaiman Mountains, runs all the way south to the Arabian Sea. Although the name Kirthar means "milk-cream," the low mountains are almost bare of vegetation. One exception is the dwarf palm tree, which is used for food and for its strong fibers. The highest mountain in the Kirthar Range rises 6,857 feet (2,090 meters). There is very little rain or snow in the region.

Western Balochistan is mostly desert. In the southwestern Makran Desert, there are active mud volcanoes. To the northwest, the Sandy Desert is home to a very small number of people. There is little farming in this barren area, and residents must move around to find grazing land for their herds. Most of the region's moisture can be found in the large areas of swampland. Because there is so little rainfall on the Balochistan plateau, irrigation works by a method called the karez system. Underground channels collect the water, which runs down from the hills and mountains. When it has traveled through the channels, the water is drawn up through shafts to water the fields. Although temperatures are very warm in this region, most of the water does not evaporate because it stays underground through its course to the fields.

THE SOUTHEASTERN DESERT

Pakistan's southeastern region, where the Sindh province lies, is dominated by the Thar Desert. Straddling the Pakistan-India border, the Thar Desert covers a total of 77,000 square miles (200,000 sq km). It also extends north into southern Punjab, where it is called the Cholistan Desert. To the south of the desert is the Rann of Kachchh (or Kutch), an area of salty mudflats, most of which belongs to India. To the west of the desert in southern Sindh are large areas of land watered by canals. Further west is the fertile valley of the Indus River.

The Thar is one of Pakistan's most desolate areas. **Monsoon** winds that sweep across the region make it even drier and bring very little rain with them. The Thar Desert is mostly made up of hills of sand or stone. One famous set of rocky hills is the Karonjhar Hills, whose name means "sprinkled with black" because their pink granite is touched with black. People have settled in flat areas between the hills of the desert and drawn on whatever resources the hills provide. The grasses that grow in the desert can be used for many purposes, including medicines and as food for grazing livestock. The desert people are also able to grow some crops by drawing from the small amount of annual rainfall and canal irriga-

A boy rides a camel across the Thar Desert at sunset. The desolate Thar is made up mostly of sand or stone.

tion systems found across the border in India.

The Thar is home to animals such as the gazelle, the black buck, and certain bird species, including the sandgrouse and the peacock. Many birds, including the Egyptian vulture, travel across the desert. It is also home to a critically endangered species known as the great Indian bustard.

INDUS RIVER PLAIN

Pakistan has a number of rivers, but its most important by far is the Indus. This great river is about 1,800 miles (2,900 km) long and passes through two places named after it—India and the Sindh province. Its present name derives from the earlier name Sindhu, which means "ocean" in ancient Sanskrit.

The Indus River rises to the east of Pakistan, in the Himalayan Mountains of Tibet. Flowing west across India's Jammu and Kashmir regions, it then curves south into Pakistan and flows in a southwesterly direction through the Punjab province. Through Sindh, it follows a gentle S-shape down to its *delta* at the Arabian Sea. Although it is much shorter than Egypt's Nile River, the world's longest river at 4,100 miles (6,600 km), its flow of water is twice as heavy. Melting water from the Himalayas, the Karakoram, and the Hindu Kush mountains swell the Indus, making navigation difficult.

The Indus Plain, which covers much of the Punjab and the Sindh provinces, is Pakistan's most productive agricultural area. The word punjab means "five waters," after the five tributaries of the Indus that run into it: the Jhelum, the Chenab, the Ravi, the Beas, and the Sutlej. In the Sindh province, the flow of the Indus becomes even heavier. During the annual floods between July and September, the plain is enriched by fertile soil from the river, and crops such as wheat, millet, rice, and cotton grow in abundance. There are also many fruit orchards in the region. The less fertile areas of the plain have artificial dams for irrigation purposes, though in many places too much salt in the water has caused problems for agriculture.

 Quick Facts: The Geography of Pakistan

Location: South Asia, bordering the Arabian Sea, between India on the east, Iran and Afghanistan on the west, and China in the north
Area: (slightly less than twice the size of California)
    total: 307,374 square miles (796,095 sq km)
    land: 297,637 square miles (770,875 sq km)
    water: 9,737 square miles (25,220 sq km)
Borders: Afghanistan, 1,659 miles (2,670 km); China, 272 miles (438 km); India, 1,982 miles (3,190 km); Iran, 596 miles (959 km)
Climate: mostly hot, dry desert; moderate in northwest, very cold in north
Terrain: flat Indus plain in east; mountains in north and northwest; Balochistan plateau in west
Elevation extremes:
    lowest point—Indian Ocean, 0 feet
    highest point—K2 (Mount Godwin-Austen), 28,656 feet (8,611 meters)
Natural hazards: frequent earthquakes, occasionally severe especially in north and west; flooding along the Indus after heavy rains (July and August)

Source: CIA World Factbook, 2015.

Motorists are stuck on a flooded street in Lahore. Flooding is common in eastern Pakistan because of the seasonal monsoon rains. In 2010, a particularly intense monsoon caused major flooding throughout Pakistan, resulted in nearly 2,000 deaths and destroying crops and homes.

The Indus delta is usually heavily flooded. It supports mangrove trees and plants that grow in swampy areas. The delta is rich in animal life, including crocodiles, dolphins, snakes, and wild boars.

CLIMATE

Pakistan is generally hot and dry, though the climates of different regions are shaped by such factors as altitude and seasonal change. It is much drier than neighboring India, where heavy rain falls for months at a time during the monsoon season.

The only region of Pakistan deeply affected by monsoon rains is the Punjab province, where land along the Indus River faces severe flooding. However, more than 75 percent of Pakistan receives less than 10 inches (25 centimeters) of rain in a year. Because of the overall dryness, much of Pakistan relies on artificial irrigation for agriculture.

Pakistan has three main seasons. The wet season, which lasts from July through September, is humid, hot, and in certain areas rainy. This season gives way to the cool season, which lasts from October through February. On the plains and in the hottest areas, such as the deserts, these months are the most pleasant of the year. The temperature in even the hottest areas usually does not go much over 70° Fahrenheit (30° Celsius). In the northern mountains, the winters can be very cold. Even in the lower heights of the mountain valleys, the temperature may drop to –4°F (–20°C). During the hot season (March through June), temperatures can rise as high as 122°F (50°C) in the desert areas, though as in all desert climates, it is much cooler at night than in the daytime. The hot season is the most pleasant in the high-altitude regions.

The monsoon winds that sweep across Pakistan have the effect of drying out the land without bringing much rain. During the summer, dust storms are a problem, especially in the hottest areas. Pakistanis may occasionally receive a refreshing break from the heat with a thunderstorm.

 ## Text-Dependent Questions

1. What four countries does Pakistan border?
2. Describe the karez system of irrigation.
3. What is the climate of the Indus Valley? How is it different from the climate of Western Balochistan?

 ## Research Project

Use the Internet or a library to learn more about the Indian bustard's status as a critically endangered species. What are the causes of the bird's population decline and what are some possible solutions?

A Pakistani woman casts her vote at a polling station in Peshawar during the 2013 election. The election was notable because it was the first time in Pakistan's history that power was transferred peacefully after the previous president served his full five-year term.

History

Thousands of years ago, the region today known as Pakistan was home to some of the world's earliest human settlements. Foreign powers later made their mark on the area, which before 1947 was considered part of India. However, no event in this region's history was more pivotal than the Arab Islamic empire's conquest in the eighth century CE, which took place only a century after the prophet Muhammad founded Islam. The religion eventually became the main factor in the formation of Pakistan.

During its modern history, Pakistan's borders have shifted more than once. These boundaries have also become flashpoints for violence and war. Even within its borders, Pakistan has been no stranger to conflict. However, the region's history began peacefully, like that of many other civilizations, with the creation of agricultural settlements on the banks of a great river.

THE INDUS VALLEY CIVILIZATION

Archaeologists believe that humans may have been raising crops in the Pakistan region as early as 7000 BCE, as peoples who formerly lived a ***nomadic*** or semi-nomadic lifestyle established permanent settlements. Mehrgarh, located in what is the Balochistan province today, may be the world's oldest urban settlement.

Beginning around 2800 BCE, the early peoples of Pakistan gradually moved eastward, toward the floodplains of the Indus River. The people of the Indus Valley civilization are sometimes called the Dravidians. They built larger settlements along the Indus, and by 2700 BCE, the Indus Valley civilization had centers in at least two major cities, Harappa and Mohenjodaro (Harappa is located in Punjab province, Mohenjodaro in Sindh province). The cities had central palaces built on hilltops, along with baths, storehouses, and homes. Archaeological evidence reveals that these people were skilled artists and craftsmen.

Words to Understand in This Chapter

Cold War—a decades-long conflict between the United States and the Soviet Union that affected diplomatic relations between their allies.

constitution—a body of principles and laws by which a state is governed.

democracy—a form of government in which the people have a say in the decision-making of the country.

dynasty—a line of rulers who pass down their authority through the family line.

nationalize—to transfer from private to state ownership.

nomadic—of a people who continually move around without a permanent home.

plebiscite—a vote by an entire electorate to express an opinion for or against a proposal or question of importance.

sanction—a measure taken by a country to force another one to obey international rules of conduct.

socialist—a theory in which the means of production, distribution, and exchange are owned by the community as a whole, rather than by private individuals or companies.

subcontinent—a major subdivision of a continent.

Turkic—relating to a group of Central Asian people who speak Altaic languages.

The remains of a stone staircase at Mohenjodaro, a city of the Indus Valley civilization that dates from the third millennium BCE.

In addition to the cities, there were also numerous smaller towns scattered throughout the region. At its peak, the Indus Valley civilization covered an area that was much larger than modern-day Pakistan and included parts of the present-day countries of India, Afghanistan, and Iran.

Around 1500 BCE, the civilization of the region changed dramatically and permanently with the arrival of the conquering Aryans. These warriors came from Central Asia and entered the Pakistan region from the north, through the Punjab. Much of what we know about the Aryans and their conquest comes from a collection of sacred texts called the Rigveda. The people were made up of several different tribes who were united under one king, although inter-tribal fighting was common. They worshiped fire, viewed cows as sacred animals, and kept themselves separate from the people they conquered by denying them privileges. The customs and beliefs of the Aryans became the foundation of the Hindu religion and its system of hereditary classes, known as castes.

Around 530 BCE, the armies of Persia claimed the entire course of the Indus River for their emperor, Cyrus the Great. Local rulers of the territory continued to govern their cities and towns, but they also had to pay tribute to the Persians. The area prospered under Persian rule for two centuries, and the towns of the Indus Valley became centers of learning and commerce.

The Persian empire was defeated around 330 BCE by the armies led by one of history's greatest military commanders—Alexander the Great, ruler of Macedonia. Alexander's conquests spread Greek culture and influence throughout his vast empire, from Egypt to Central Asia. There was no strong central authority in the Pakistan region to stop Alexander from taking control of the province in 326 BCE. However, by the time the ruler's army reached as far east as India, the soldiers did not want to go any further, and in 325 Alexander retreated from Pakistan.

The Greeks maintained only nominal control over the region for about two decades. In 305 BCE the Mauryan empire of India took control of the Indus Valley. This empire, founded by Chandragupta Maurya, was the first of India's great ruling powers. It lasted for about 100 years, building a strong economy in the India and Pakistan regions. The empire retreated from Pakistan, however, after dissension and unrest weakened its leadership.

Over the next few centuries, a series of powerful peoples fought for control of Pakistan. The Bactrian empire, founded by Greeks in Central Asia, took over the Indus River valley in 185 BCE. Control then passed to the Scythians, a nomadic tribe from Central Asia. From Persia, the Parthians took northern Pakistan around the year 7 CE. However, none of these empires had much long-term impact on the Pakistan region.

Another Central Asian power, the Kushan **dynasty**, conquered northern Pakistan around the year 60 CE, ruling for about 300 years. This empire, which at its height encompassed modern-day Tajikistan, Pakistan, and Afghanistan, had one of its capitals in Peshawar (today a major city in northern Pakistan). The Kushans carried on trade with the other major empires of the day, including the Roman Empire. They also helped to make Buddhism one of the major religions in Central Asia.

The Gupta Empire, which followed the Kushans, was one of the greatest in India's history. At the empire's height, around the year 400, Hinduism had become the most important religion in India. Although the Gupta Empire never ruled directly over the Pakistan region, it maintained a strong cultural and religious influence over its neighbors to the west.

Over the next few hundred years, various tribes overran South Asia and Pakistan. They included the Gurjaras of India and the Huns. The most successful Hun campaigns were made by the White Huns, also known as the Hephthalites. The Huns' exact origins are unknown, but experts believe that they may have come from the Iran region or elsewhere in Central Asia. Especially in Europe, where they devastated powerful empires and kingdoms, they became known as strong warriors who subdued their enemies with ferocity. Many of the tribes of modern Pakistan are probably descended from the Huns.

THE COMING OF ISLAM

The arrival of Islam was a turning point in the history of Pakistan and of the entire **subcontinent**. The introduction of the religion was the first step toward Muslim ascendancy in South Asia, and the initial divide between Islam and Hinduism eventually led to the division of India and the creation of Pakistan.

The Islamic faith was introduced to the peoples of the Arabian

(Top) The fabled Khyber Pass, through which Arab armies brought Islam to Pakistan and northern India. (Inset) This example of decorative Pakistani calligraphy is the shahada, or Muslim profession of faith: "There is no god but Allah, and Muhammad is His messenger."

Peninsula by the Prophet Muhammad. Around the year 613 Muhammad began sharing the revelations he received from God (called Allah). Although Muhammad's followers were originally persecuted, their numbers and military strength gradually increased. By the time of Muhammad's death in 632, Muslims controlled much of the Arabian Peninsula. Driven to spread their religion and expand their control, the Arabs conquered neighboring territories controlled by the Persian and Byzantine Empires. By 650, the Arabs had overthrown the Sassanid dynasty in Persia and incorporated its territories into the growing Muslim empire. In the years following its defeat, the people of Persia converted to Islam.

The Muslims continued to expand west into Europe and North Africa and east into Central Asia. In 711, the Arab general

Muhammad bin Qasim invaded Sindh. By 712, he had taken Sindh's most important port, Daibul. From 750 until 962, Sindh was ruled by governors serving the Abbasids, an Arab Muslim dynasty of caliphs who ruled from the city of Baghdad, in present-day Iraq.

The Abbasid rulers encouraged much cross-cultural exchange. Many Arab scholars traveled east to Pakistan and India, while Hindu scholars traveled to Baghdad. As a result, the two groups often shared what they knew about medicine, mathematics, and other subjects. Arab culture had a great impact on the everyday life and language of the people of the Sindh region. Even today, for example, the Sindhi language still contains many Arabic words.

Although the people of Sindh and other parts of South Asia were subject to Muslim rule after the eighth century, they were not forced to convert to Islam. However, many people—especially those who belonged to the lower Hindu castes—chose to convert because in contrast to the Hindu system, Islam at least promised social and economic equality.

In the latter part of the 10th century, the Abbasid Empire began to decline. Control over South Asia gradually passed to the Ghaznavids, a dynasty of **Turkic** rulers previously under the rule of the Abbasids. In 998, Mahmud, one of the first Ghaznavid rulers, became the first Muslim ruler to take the title of sultan. During the rule of the Ghaznavids over the region, the mystical Muslim sect known as the Sufis became very influential.

The Abbasids and the Ghaznavids had used Turkic slave-soldiers, known as Mamluks (from the Arab word for "owned") to help them rule. Eventually the Mamluks seized power for themselves. In 1211 Mamluk general Qutb ud-Din proclaimed himself sultan of Delhi, an important city of India. He established the first ruling dynasty of what became known as the Delhi Sultanate. By the mid-13th century, the Delhi Sultanate was the strongest Muslim power in South Asia.

The Mamluks lost control over the Delhi Sultanate around 1290, and were supplanted by other ruling dynasties: the Khilji (1290–1320), Tughlaq (1320–1413), Sayyid (1414–51), and Lodhi (1451–1526). However, throughout this time the powerful Delhi Sultanate remained the center for Muslim control over practically all of Pakistan and much of modern-day India.

The laws of the Delhi Sultanate were based on the Qur'an, the holy scriptures of Islam, and on traditional Muslim rules and principles; however, non-Muslims were permitted to practice their religion as long as they paid an additional tax to the state. Because of this tolerance, Islamic and Indian culture could be combined to create great works of literature, music, and architecture.

The sultanate did face external pressures, however. The Mongols had been moving west across Asia, ruthlessly killing those who stood in their way, and by 1221 the Mongol ruler Genghis Khan had reached the Indus River. By the time of Genghis's death six years later, the Mongols ruled an enormous empire that stretched from China to Europe. Yet the Delhi Sultanate was not destroyed, and its armies fought back the invading Mongols on several occasions. Although the Mongols sacked Lahore in 1240, they were never really able to shake the control of the sultans in India. (Ultimately, Islam emerged victorious in the conflict; by 1313 the Mongols had converted and made Islam the official religion of their empire.)

In the late 14th century, a conqueror who claimed descent from Genghis Khan succeeded where the Mongols had failed. Timur Lenk (known in the West as Tamerlane) led an army that sacked Delhi in 1398. Timur built a vast empire in Asia, but he had a reputation as a bloodthirsty conqueror—in Delhi his army massacred some 80,000 people.

Timur eventually withdrew from South Asia, and the weakened sultanate reemerged as a regional power. Delhi returned to prominence in India under the rule of the Lodhi dynasty, but in the 16th century one of Timur's descendants, Babur, would conquer Delhi and add it to his own vast South Asian empire.

RISE OF THE MUGHAL EMPIRE

The Mughal Empire, one of the greatest in Central Asian history, dominated the Indian subcontinent and the Pakistan region from the 16th to the 18th century. During this long reign, some of the region's greatest monuments were built.

Babur, a Turkic ruler, founded the Mughal Empire. Born in 1483 in the Central Asian kingdom of Fergana, Babur claimed descent from both Genghis Khan and Timur. He made his first important conquest in 1504, when he took Kabul, in modern-day Afghanistan. In 1524, he conquered Lahore; only two years later, he overthrew the last ruler of the Delhi Sultanate.

Along with becoming famous for their conquests, the Mughal rulers were also known for their promotion of the arts and the beautiful buildings they constructed. Akbar, one of the greatest Mughal rulers, reigned from 1556 to 1605. He extended the empire and improved the way it was governed. The level of religious free-

Some of the region's most notable buildings were constructed during the rule of the Mughal Empire. An example of the best Mughal architecture is the Badshahi Mosque, with its simple lines and pleasing proportions. The mosque was built during the rule of Aurangzeb, the last great Mughal emperor; during his reign (1658–1707), the empire achieved its greatest military strength and conquered several neighboring Hindu kingdoms.

dom sanctioned by Akbar was unprecedented. He married both Muslim and Hindu wives, and also explored the beliefs of many different religions, including Christianity. Another Mughal emperor, Shah Jahan, was famous for the buildings he commissioned. During his rule from 1627 to 1658, he built the famous Taj Mahal as a tomb for his wife and had the colorful Wazir Khan's Mosque constructed as a major site of Muslim worship.

In an empire in which a minority group of Muslims ruled a Hindu majority, religious tolerance was particularly important. Unfortunately, some of the Mughal rulers who came after Akbar were far less tolerant of other religions. This created a greater division between Muslims and non-Muslims than ever before.

THE BRITISH IN INDO-PAKISTAN

Mughal emperors continued to rule until 1857, although their influence was greatly weakened by the arrival of the British, who during the 17th century began to form trade relationships with local rulers in Pakistan and India. Typically, Mughal emperors were allowed to keep their titles, but in reality most emperors served the interests of the British, who sought to gain control of the entire subcontinent.

The British arrived in India at a time when all major European nations were establishing colonies around the world, including the Middle East and Asia. Colonialism allowed the ruling families of Europe to profit from the wealth and the resources available in other parts of the world. Others countries had already tried to gain a foothold on the subcontinent. The Portuguese first arrived in India in 1498; they were followed by the Dutch and the French. Representatives of the British East India Company began establishing trade around 1600. With the full support of the British government, this company gained exclusive trading rights in India. Throughout the 17th and the 18th century, the British continued to gain the monopoly on trade, suppressing Indian resistance while winning campaigns against their European rivals. Their control expanded greatly with a victory in 1757 at the Battle of Plassey, a conflict over the lucrative trade region of Bengal in eastern India. By 1784, the year the British government passed the India Act, British dominance of the region was complete, with the East India Company the foundation of its rule.

It took longer for the British to gain control in the Pakistan region. People living in the Punjab were united by the Sikh religion, founded by Guru Nanak in the late 15th century. Through their triumphs over the ruling Mughal Empire in the early 19th century, the Sikhs proved their military might. One very prominent ruler of the Punjab was Ranjit Singh, who led a large army that had some of the most modern weaponry in the continent. Singh conquered Lahore in 1799 and took the title of *maharaja*, or "great ruler." He later conquered Kashmir in 1819 and Peshawar in 1834.

The Mughal emperor Shah Alum grants Robert Clive of the British East India Company authority to administer the Bengal, Bihar, and Orissa provinces of India. This concession, which followed British military successes at the battles of Plassey (1757) and Buxar (1764), opened the way for greater British involvement in the region.

In general, the British let Ranjit Singh rule the Punjab as he pleased. However, after his death in 1839, the British made their bid for control. The Sindh region fell early to the British in 1843. The Sikh Wars (1845–46 and 1849), in which the Sikhs of the Punjab tried unsuccessfully to halt the advance of the British armies, ended with their inclusion in the British Empire. Ironically, following the resolution of the second Sikh War, the Punjab would become one of the most supportive provinces of British rule.

Other areas created more problems for the British. The British fought fierce battles with the Baloch and the Pathans, tribes who lived on the borders of Afghanistan. The conflicts became known as the First Afghan War (1839–42) and the Second Afghan War (1878–80). Both wars ended unsuccessfully for the British, who temporarily gave up efforts to conquer these remote territories.

The Hindu ruler of Kashmir allowed the British safe passage through Kashmir during their war to pacify Afghanistan in 1841. He also supported the British against the Sikhs, a favor the British rewarded by granting him permanent control of the predominantly Muslim region. This decision initiated a war between Hindus and Muslims over Kashmir that has continued into modern times.

From early on, the British showed a lack of sensitivity to the religious practices of the empire's Hindus and Muslims. This prejudice fueled several rebellions. One such insurgency was the Indian Mutiny of 1857, a military uprising that quickly developed into widespread rebellion. Many Indian Hindu and Muslim soldiers in the British army became angry when they were given new rifle cartridges that were wrapped in paper greased with beef and pork fat. Because their religions forbid Hindus from eating beef and Muslims from eating pork, this was deemed an offensive violation of religious law.

Although the issue of the rifle cartridges was the immediate cause of the Indian Mutiny, there were other issues that went much deeper. Some Muslims and Hindus felt threatened by the increasing activity of Christian missionaries in the subcontinent and the general intolerance demonstrated by the British.

The revolt was contained by 1859, though not before rebels took the city of Delhi and proclaimed Mughal emperor Bahadur Shah II to be the ruler of India. The Muslim soldiers of Punjab showed their allegiance to the British army by helping take Delhi back from the rebels.

There were several significant outcomes of the Indian Mutiny—the most obvious of them was the formal end of the Mughal Empire as well as the end of East India Company rule. Replacing these two entities was the British Raj, a new form of government that enabled Britain to more directly govern the subcontinent. With the colonial power's place in the region secured, India become known as "the jewel in the crown" of the empire.

Another consequence of the rebellion was that the British began to treat members of different religious groups unequally. In India, the Hindus gained position, while the Muslims, to whom the British assigned most of the blame for the mutiny, faced persecution and were robbed of their property. This was not the case in the Punjab, however, where most Muslims had supported the British for a long time and received rewards for their loyalty. The Muslims continued to dominate the northwest region of British India—modern-day Pakistan—with the blessing of the British government.

In the areas that would later become Pakistan's Khyber Pakhtunkhwa Province and Balochistan, the British still struggled against the Pathan and Baloch tribes. By 1896, the British had drawn the Durand Line, adding parts—but not all—of the Pathan tribal areas to British India. The Pathans revolted the following year, and thousands of British troops were sent to put down the rebellion. In 1901, Khyber Pakhtunkhwa was officially created as the North-West Frontier Province so it could be ruled more closely by a local administration.

Movements Toward Independence

During the second half of the 19th century, a growing number of Indians pushed for independence from Britain. British leaders made a few concessions, giving Indians limited leadership positions on the provincial and national level.

Muslims in British India made similar demands. However, they worried that if India became independent, the larger Hindu community might oppress Muslims. Sayyid Ahmad Khan, an Indian Muslim leader during this period, voiced the anxiety of the Muslim community: "Suppose all the English were to leave India, then who would be the rulers of India? It is necessary that one of them—[Islam] and Hinduism—should conquer the other and thrust it down."

In 1885, the Indian National Congress was formed. While this political party was the foremost group of those advocating freedom, its membership did not accurately reflect the views of Muslims: at the party's first meeting, only two of the 73 representatives were Muslim, while 54 were upper-caste Hindus.

Mohandas Gandhi, a Hindu lawyer famed for his philosophy of nonviolent resistance, became the voice of the Indian independence movement during the 1920s. Meanwhile, during this time the movement for a completely separate Muslim homeland also began to take shape. Two prominent Muslims, the lawyer Mohammed Ali Jinnah and the poet and politician Dr. Allama Muhammad Iqbal, became leaders of this movement.

Jinnah initially entered politics as a member of the Indian National Congress. His goal from the beginning was the end of British domination in the subcontinent. Originally, he believed that the way to reach this goal was by uniting Indian members of different religions and cultures against the British. One of his Hindu supporters even called him "the best ambassador of Hindu-Muslim unity." Jinnah helped to bring the Indian National Congress and the Muslim League closer than they had ever been before. However, when he became disillusioned by the Hindus' reluctance to give Muslims an equal share in politics, he left the Indian National Congress in 1920. After his wife died in 1929, he moved to England.

In 1930, Iqbal made a famous speech at a meeting of the Muslim League in which he formally introduced the idea of a separate Muslim state. This plan was eagerly supported by a group of Muslim students at Cambridge University in England, who came up with a name for this homeland—Pakistan, "the land of the pure."

THE CREATION OF PAKISTAN

The idea of a new Muslim state had a powerful influence on Jinnah's thinking, and he exchanged a number of letters with Iqbal. In one of them, Iqbal wrote, "You are the only Muslim in India today to whom the community has a right to look up for safe guidance through the storm which is coming to North-West India, and perhaps to the whole of India." Inspired to rejoin the freedom movement, Jinnah returned from England in 1935. Once again, he hoped that the Muslim League and the Congress could coordinate their efforts. However, when the British permitted the Indian

These posters picture two of the leaders who advocated for the creation of a separate Muslim country in India during the early 20th century, the philosopher-poet Allama Muhammad Iqbal (1877–1938) and politician Mohammed Ali Jinnah (1876–1948).

National Congress to elect its own provincial governments in 1937, the INC prohibited the election of members of the Muslim League. With this final blow, Jinnah gave up on the idea of Muslim-Hindu cooperation.

In March 1940, the Muslim League held a meeting in Lahore at which Jinnah presented the Lahore Resolution (later called the Pakistan Resolution). The statement proclaimed that "Muslims are a nation and according to any definition of a nation they must have their homelands, their territory, their state." The resolution called for the creation of a new state for Muslims in British India, ruled by Islamic principles.

During the 1940s, violence mounted between Muslims and Hindus in India as their relations worsened. India's Hindu government continued to oppose the idea of a divided India, but the British saw the creation of a separate Muslim homeland as the only way forward. They chose August 14, 1947, as the date of partition, and it was agreed that before that day each province had to decide whether to become part of independent India or Pakistan.

The western Muslim provinces and the eastern province of Bengal voted to become part of Pakistan. Because over 1,000 miles (1,600 km) separated Bengal from the western territories, the country was divided as East Pakistan and West Pakistan.

Jammu and Kashmir, a state with a Muslim majority ruled by a Hindu prince, remained a contested territory. In October 1947, the Pakistani army joined Pathan rebels as they advanced toward Srinagar, the capital of Jammu and Kashmir. The prince then asked India for assistance, which it gave—but on the condition that Kashmir join the Indian union. When the accord was signed, Indian prime minister Jawaharlal Nehru sent in thousands of troops to defend what was now officially Indian territory. The First Kashmir War lasted through 1948, with heavy losses on both sides. Eventually, the United Nations negotiated a cease-fire and arranged

Hindu and Muslim leaders meet with Lord Louis Mountbatten, Britain's viceroy of India, at a June 1947 conference in New Delhi. Pictured are (left to right) Indian nationalist leader Jawaharlal Nehru, British adviser Lord Ismay, Mountbatten, and president of the All-India Muslim League Mohammed Ali Jinnah. During this meeting, Mountbatten disclosed Britain's partition plan for India.

for a ***plebiscite*** to determine the future of the entire province. The vote was never held, however, and the problem of Kashmir would continue to haunt Pakistan and India.

The partition of British India resulted in fighting in the Punjab as well as Jammu and Kashmir. Millions of Muslims in the new state of India fled as refugees for Pakistan, while millions of Hindus left the Pakistan territories for India. In a frenzy of anger, both Muslims and Hindus killed each other as they tried to escape to safety. No one knows the exact numbers, but most estimates put the death toll at a million people. The tragic events of 1947–48 set a pattern of aggression between Pakistan and India that has continued to the present day.

PAKISTAN'S EARLY YEARS

Mohammed Ali Jinnah was Pakistan's first governor-general. By this point, he also had the title of Quaid-i-Azam, or "Great Leader." The country's first prime minister was Liaquat Ali Khan.

The new state faced many challenges. Shortly after partition, Pakistan faced significant debt. It had begun statehood with an extremely limited economy, and military spending was already cut-

Liaquat Ali Khan (1896–1951) was the first prime minister of Pakistan; he is pictured here (at left) standing with Jinnah outside the Indian Office in London.

ting down the national budget. In addition to these basic problems, war over Kashmir broke out almost immediately.

Jinnah died of tuberculosis in September 1948. After the loss of Pakistan's Great Leader, Liaquat Ali Khan was challenged to keep moving the country forward. The prime minister worked toward drafting a democratic **constitution** that emphasized the Islamic ideals of Pakistan. His work was left unfinished, however, as he was assassinated in October 1951. The constitution would be ratified five years later.

During the 1950s, Pakistan was politically divided by the demands of militant Muslims, who felt that the government was making too many compromises. East Pakistanis were also unhappy over many issues, including the decision to make Urdu the official language of both parts of Pakistan. They saw this as an insult to their identity, because Bengali was their first language. A group of the dissenters, the United Front Party, grew in popularity and routed the Muslim League in East Pakistan's general elections in 1954. Following the election, tensions between the two parts of Pakistan continued to grow. The country's struggling economy and the threat of famine intensified these disagreements.

Pakistan's constitution, ratified in 1956, declared the country an Islamic republic. General Iskander Mirza became Pakistan's first elected president. However, attempts to make Pakistan a **democracy** did not fare well. Conflicts between the different political parties, regions, and ethnic groups were steadily weakening the country. In October 1958, a military coup overthrew Mirza, and he was forced to go into exile. The country's new leader, General Muhammad Ayub Khan, firmly believed in a unified Pakistan. However, he thought it necessary to establish martial law, or rule by the army. The fact that Punjabis heavily populated the military made the other Pakistani ethnic groups even more dissatisfied.

Ayub Khan's government implemented many reforms. Under his rule, there was a great deal of economic growth. Business, industry, and agriculture all improved. Aided by training and equipment from the United States, the Pakistani army also grew stronger. But the changes and improvements did not ease the tension between economic classes and various ethnic groups. Ayub Khan's land reforms were supposed to more fairly distribute the farmlands; however, they did not benefit the poor, and the middle and upper classes only became richer. More and more jobs and positions of power went to Punjabis and Pathans. The Muhajirs, who had fled to Pakistan from India after the partition, became increasingly disadvantaged.

During the 1960s, Pakistan's relations with both India and Afghanistan worsened. The Afghan and Pathan tribes along Pakistan's western border continued to push for an independent state of their own, leading to a breakdown of relations between the two countries. The Second Kashmir War between India and Pakistan broke out in 1965. It lasted for only two and a half months, though when the fighting ended the two countries were no closer to resolving the border conflict.

After the war, discontent over Ayub Khan's leadership increased. Following an attempt on his life, he resigned and handed over power to General Agha Mohammad Yahya Khan. Yahya wanted to bring democracy back to Pakistan. He arranged for general elections to be held in 1970. However, the elections had serious consequences. In East Pakistan, the Bengali-led Awami League won an overwhelming majority, while the Pakistan People's Party (PPP), led by Zulfikar Ali Bhutto, won the majority in West Pakistan. Since East Pakistan had the larger population, the Awami League claimed the right to lead the Pakistani government.

Threatened by the Awami League's rise to power, Yahya moved to ban the party, which responded by declaring East Pakistan a separate state in March 1971. West Pakistani troops invaded and occupied East Pakistan, placing it under martial law. Millions of Bengalis fled from East Pakistan into India, and hundreds of thousands of others died in the civil war. In December, India sent troops into East Pakistan. The short conflict led to the loss of much of Pakistan's army. It also led to East Pakistan becoming an independent country, Bangladesh (which means "Bengal Land").

YEARS OF POLITICAL INSTABILITY

The loss of East Pakistan was a terrible blow to Pakistan. Yahya resigned and was replaced by Zulfikar Ali Bhutto, who enjoyed initial popularity as an advocate for the nation's poor. His slogan was Roti, Kapra, aur Makan (Bread, Clothes, and Housing). In many ways, the new government was based on **socialist** principles, and Bhutto **nationalized** banks and major industries. In 1973, the national assembly adopted a new constitution and Bhutto became prime minister.

However, Bhutto's government became increasingly like a dictatorship. He began removing all government officials who opposed him in any way. He also established a watchdog group called the Federal Security Force (FSF). The FSF created an atmosphere of fear, and its members are believed to have killed some of Bhutto's political opponents. During the 1970s, he forcibly took away property from owners in most industry sectors. He even imprisoned major businessmen and took away their passports. In 1973, Bhutto accused the Balochistan government of planning to separate from Pakistan.

Soldiers of Pakistan's army on during the Bengali war for independence, 1971. Although the people of East and West Pakistan were predominantly Muslims, there were many cultural, geographic, and economic differences between the regions. East Pakistan seceded in March 1971, declaring itself the independent state of Bangladesh. A civil war ensued; with India's assistance, Bangladesh won the war in December 1971. An estimated 1 million Bengalis were killed during the fighting; millions more took refuge in India. In 1974, Pakistan official-ly recognized Bangladesh as an independent nation.

When he closed down the provincial government and sent armed forces into the area, the resulting riots killed thousands of people.

While Bhutto's economic policies were supposedly founded on socialism, in reality they just benefited the upper classes of Pakistan. Most of the wealthy kept their powerful positions, while the situations of the middle classes and the poor hardly improved.

Bhutto's determination to keep his power at all costs ultimately ended in his undoing. In 1977, he called a national election. Although several groups combined to form a major opposition party known as the Pakistan National Alliance (PNA), the PPP still remained the most popular party. Had Bhutto not interfered with the voting process, he probably would have safely won the election with enough votes, but in addition to ordering officials to remove

When the government of Zulfikar Ali Bhutto (1928–1979) grew more authoritarian, it was overthrown by Pakistan's military.

opponents from the list of candidates, Bhutto had his FSF and the police break up meetings of the opposition parties.

When Bhutto and the PPP won the election by a huge majority, the PNA raised the accusations of vote tampering. Bhutto responded by arresting and executing his accusers. Seeing that the country was approaching chaos, he then sent the army into Pakistan's major cities to suppress revolt. However, the military turned against Bhutto, and the chief of staff, General Muhammad Zia ul-Haq, arrested Bhutto and imposed martial law.

When the dictator was later released, it quickly became obvious that he was still very popular. Because he was anxious about losing his new position of power, Zia had Bhutto arrested again. This time, Bhutto was indicted for the attempted murder of one of his opponents. The Lahore High Court sentenced him to death. Countries all over the world asked for Bhutto's life to be spared, but Pakistan's government followed through with the sentence, executing him by hanging in April 1979.

Hoping to secure support for his new government from Pakistan's powerful Muslim leaders, Zia made several drastic moves. After the execution of Bhutto, he arrested thousands of PPP supporters and declared that all political parties were illegal. One of the main features of Zia's rule was a leaning toward a more Islamic form of government.

Muslim leaders had demanded that the legal system be revised to conform to Sharia, a body of regulations that is based on the Qur'an, the holy book of Islam, and on the example of the Prophet

Muhammad and his companions. Zia did not accede to all their demands, but he did appoint a body called the Islamic Ideology Council. This assembly changed or abolished many existing laws, based on whether or not they conformed to Sharia. Islamic criminal laws, with penalties that included floggings and stoning, became national law in 1979.

Other countries, especially in the Western world, were critical of Zia's harsh policies—at least until the Soviet Union invaded Afghanistan in December 1979. In keeping with its **Cold War** agenda, the United States supported Afghanistan against its Soviet opponents. Zia declared that Pakistan would help its neighbor, and by hosting Afghan refugees of the war and supporting resistance fighters known as mujahideen, the country suddenly became a key ally of the Western world. During the Soviet-Afghan War, which lasted until 1989, about 3 million people fled into Pakistan, which was rewarded for its assistance with an enormous amount of financial aid from the United States.

Zia introduced several more measures that sought to bring the country more in line with Islamic principles. He called for interest-free banking, in keeping with prohibitions in the Qur'an against charging interest. He also ordered the revision of school textbooks so they would have more Islamic content, and expected government officials to encourage people to pray five times a day. In 1984, Zia asked for a referendum vote on the new Islamic measures. The referendum also stood as an election to place Zia in power for five

Muhammad Zia ul-Haq (1924–1988) performs one of the five daily prayers required of devout Muslims. As president of Pakistan, Zia issued laws and decrees that brought the country more in line with Islamic teaching.

more years. Although very few people turned out at the polls, a large majority of those who did voted for Zia and his policies.

Meanwhile, growing ethnic tensions made the country increasingly unstable. In 1983, thousands died or were imprisoned during fighting in Sindh, where the Sindhis felt that they were losing ground to other ethnic groups. In 1986, there was serious rioting in Karachi, Quetta, and Hyderabad, caused by tensions between the Muhajirs and the Pathans. By this time, ethnic violence had become one of Pakistan's most serious problems.

In August 1988, Zia and 30 others died in a plane crash. Many Pakistanis saw the tragedy as an opportunity for the country to move forward. "Zia's death has removed the shadow under which myself and all those dedicated to democracy have been living," said Benazir Bhutto, the daughter of Zulfikar Ali Bhutto and the head of the PPP. When new elections were held, Benazir Bhutto became Pakistan's new prime minister, or head of government. Ghulam Ishaq Khan became the president, or head of state, which at that time in Pakistan was a less-powerful position than that of prime minister. Bhutto was the first woman ever to become the political leader of a Muslim state.

Benazir Bhutto's first government only lasted for less than two years. Outsiders perceived her government as a return to democracy. They also believed that the rise to power of a woman was a sign of exciting changes in the Muslim world. Within Pakistan, however, people were not as impressed. Bhutto's government did little to stimulate the country's failing economy or to reduce Pakistan's massive debt. An alliance between the PPP and a militant party known as the Muhajir Qaumi Movement (MQM) further destabilized the government. Ethnic violence worsened throughout the country, especially in Sindh where the MQM was centered.

During Bhutto's rule, tension over Kashmir rose dramatically. In 1989 militant Islamic groups increased their demands that India give up its claim to the region, and Bhutto's government called for azadi ("freedom") for the people of Kashmir. Both countries moved forces into position in the Kashmir region. Although major fighting did not break out at the time, relations between India and Pakistan worsened.

By this point, Bhutto was facing accusations of corruption and the abuse of power. Pakistan's president, Ghulam Ishaq Khan, removed Bhutto from office in August 1990. (Although Pakistan's president generally had less power, the constitution gave him or her the power to dismiss the prime minister.) Khan replaced Bhutto with Nawaz Sharif, the head of the Islamic Democratic Alliance (IJI).

Benazir Bhutto (1953–2007) was elected prime minister after Zia's death in 1988. She promised that under her government Pakistan would again become a secular democracy, but economic problems and reports of corruption led to her removal in 1990. After facing trial for abuse of power, Bhutto was reelected as prime minister, serving from 1993 to 1996

Sharif's government lasted until 1993. He improved Pakistan's economy by privatizing many industries and encouraging imports and exports with other countries. Like Muhammad Zia ul-Haq, Sharif directed Parliament to place more weight on Islamic law. However, Sharif made the mistake of trying to reduce the president's power. In 1993, the president dismissed Sharif in almost exactly the same way that he had dismissed Bhutto. In the end, the military pressured both Sharif and Ishaq Khan to resign. Following Sharif's resignation, Benazir Bhutto returned to power in the 1993 elections.

During Bhutto's second term in office, Pakistan's situation worsened. In 1995, the ethnic violence had increased to such a level that the government allowed the police forces to perform execution-style killings of those involved. The economy steadily declined, and by June 1997 the country had a debt of more than $34 billion. In 1996, Bhutto was once again dismissed from office. After Nawaz Sharif was reelected prime minister in the 1997 elections, one of his first moves was to amend the constitution so that the president could no longer dismiss the government at will.

PAKISTAN ENTERS THE NUCLEAR AGE

Sharif was eager to help Pakistan escape the problems that had crippled it during the 1980s and 1990s. With the help of institutions such as the International Monetary Fund and the World Bank, he worked to reduce Pakistan's debt and to improve the economy. He ended the Muslim League's alliance with the radical MQM after a series of violent MQM-related incidents. However, internal power struggles weakened Sharif's government.

In May 1998, tensions escalated again in South Asia when India tested nuclear weapons in the state of Rajasthan. Two weeks later, Pakistan tested its own nuclear weapons in Balochistan.

Although international intelligence agencies such as the CIA were shocked when the tests were conducted, Pakistan's nuclear program had existed for decades. In 1990 the United States had imposed **sanctions** to try to force Pakistan to discontinue working on nuclear weapons. Following the tests in 1998, the U.S. imposed economic sanctions on India as well.

The ongoing Kashmir dispute escalated into what became known as the Kargil conflict in the summer of 1999. Battles raged along the Line of Control, a disputed border between Pakistan and India through the Kashmir region. Pakistan sent troops into Indian Kashmir, but withdrew under international pressure. The region remained unstable, however. When U.S. President Bill Clinton visited India in March 2000, he called Kashmir "the most dangerous place in the world."

In October 1999, Sharif's government fell after a failed attempt to remove his military chief, General Pervez Musharraf. The armed forces, which had sided with Musharraf against Sharif, made the general president of Pakistan. After the coup, which took place without violence, Musharraf announced that the armed forces would take action to prevent "further destabilization"—meaning Pakistan was once again under military rule. Although the Western world was unhappy with what it perceived as Pakistan's return to a dictatorship, most Pakistanis welcomed Musharraf's takeover. In the years leading up to the coup, conditions had worsened in Pakistan and the government had proven to be ineffective and corrupt.

Pervez Musharraf was the head of Pakistan's army before he seized power in the fall of 1999; over the next few years he assumed practically all authority over the government before stepping down under pressure in August 2008.

Enormous military spending continued to keep Pakistan deep in debt, but with the country continually mired in conflict, a large military budget seemed necessary. In late 2001, following bombings in Indian Kashmir and Delhi, India broke off its relations with Pakistan. Both countries braced for war, with more than a million troops stationed along the Line of Control for over a year. For a few months, nuclear war in South Asia seemed like a strong possibility. But thanks in large part to diplomatic efforts by the United States and several other countries, in April 2003 India's prime minister, Atal Bihari Vajpayee, moved to restore relations with Pakistan, and in November of that year a cease-fire was declared.

Although relations between the two countries have improved,

animosity between India and Pakistan remains. In recent years, terrorist attacks such as a series of deadly shootings in Mumbai, India, during November 2008, and a bombing at a police station in the disputed state of Jumma and Kashmir, India, have slowed the peace process. This is primarily because the government in New Delhi has claimed it believes the attacks were carried out by groups secretly supported by Pakistan's government. Pakistan is frequently criticized for not doing enough to stop terrorist groups within its borders.

GOVERNMENTAL CHANGES

Pakistan returned to constitutional government in 2002. In the same year, Musharraf won a referendum that extended his presidency another five years. As leader he drew his share of controversy. Accusations of fraud accompanied the 2002 election, and in December 2003 there were two separate attempts on Musharraf's life. Just a few months later, Pakistani scientists admitted that in the 1990s they sold nuclear secrets to Libya and North Korea—countries that Western governments wanted to keep from developing nuclear weapons because they have supported international terrorism.

Musharraf encountered more challenges when, in 2007, the Supreme Court ruled that former prime minister Nawaz Sharif could return to Pakistan from exile in Saudi Arabia. Facing challenges from Sharif and former prime minister Benazir Bhutto, Musharraf initially agreed to a power-sharing agreement that had him relinquish his post as chief of the army so he could run for reelection as president. However, Musharraf soon changed his proposal, claiming that he would step down as army chief if elected to another term as president.

In November 2007, Musharraf declared a state of emergency and suspended the constitution. He also fired the judges of the Supreme Court. Many felt that Musharraf was trying to prevent the court from declaring that he could not constitutionally run for president while head of the military. In protest, thousands of lawyers took to the streets; hundreds were arrested.

After eight years in exile, Nawaz Sharif returned to Pakistan in November 2007. He demanded that emergency rule be lifted and that the Supreme Court justices be reinstated. Later that month, Musharraf stepped down as military chief. In December, Musharraf ended emergency rule and restored the Constitution—but not before he made sure no one could challenge what he had done during the period of emergency rule.

In 2013, Nawaz Sharif was elected prime minister of Pakistan for an unprecedented third term. He previously served in that position from 1990 to 1993, and from 1997 to 1999.

In late 2007, Benazir Bhutto was assassinated in a suicide attack during a campaign rally in Rawalpindi. While President Musharraf blamed al Qaeda for the attack, others—including most of Bhutto's supporters—accused Musharraf's government of involvement with the attack.

With impeachment pressure mounting, Musharraf agreed to step down from his post on August 18, 2008. He was succeeded by Asif Ali Zardari, Benazir Bhutto's husband.

One of the prominent themes of Zardari's administration was opposition to Islamic terrorist groups. Zardari supported the United States and NATO for their anti-terrorist actions in Pakistan, a controversial position at home. Many Pakistanis oppose U.S. drone attacks, which sometimes result in the accidental deaths of Pakistani civilians. Yet the U.S. and NATO gained ground against terrorist groups. In 2009, the United States killed the leader of Pakistan's Taliban in South Waziristan. In 2011, U.S. special forces

Asif Ali Zardari, elected president in 2008, is the first democratically elected president of Pakistan to complete his five-year term. However, he was criticized in Pakistan for his government's support of U.S. military operations in the region, as well as for his administration's slow response to a major flooding crisis in 2010. Zardari decided not to run for president in 2013.

killed al Qaeda leader Osama bin Laden in the Pakistani town of Abbottabad. The raid of foreign soldiers within Pakistan's borders earned Zardari intense criticism from Pakistanis.

Zardari's government conducted its own operations against terrorists in the country, yet the president was criticized for not doing enough. A suicide bombing in Peshawar killed 120 people in 2009, the same year that a string of political killings and bombings occurred in Karachi. Violence continued with attacks against the Shia minority group in Rawalpindi and Quetta. In 2012, Taliban gunmen shot 14-year-old Malala Yousafzai, who was speaking out for girls' right to education. Malala survived the attack and fled to England. She has continued to promote girls' education in Pakistan, earning the Nobel Peace Prize in 2014.

Zardari also received criticism for the weak government response to extreme flooding in 2010, which killed at least 1,600 people and affected more than 20 million. The president was also accused of corruption and mismanaging the economy.

However, Zardari made steps toward a more democratic Pakistan, including revising the constitution to eliminate changes made by the military dictators of the past. Zardari even agreed to an amendment that transferred some of his presidential powers to the prime minister.

In 2013, Zardari became the first democratically elected president to complete a full five-year term. That same year, a peaceful transfer of power occurred when Mamnoon Hussain was elected as Pakistan's new president. Nawaz Sharif, who had been re-elected to the legislature in 2008, led his party to victory and was elected to the office of prime minister for an unprecedented third time. Despite terrorist violence and intimidation tactics aimed at keeping people from the polls, more voters showed up than in any election since 1970. Sharif's Muslim League party won the majority of votes with promises of an improved economy, military reforms, and peace with India. Yet, Sharif's ambitious agenda has seen little progress and instability continues. Protests led by opposition leaders nearly shut down the government in 2014, and violence by the Taliban and other extremist groups continues.

 Text-Dependent Questions

1. How did the Hindu religion come to the Indus Valley?
2. Describe the impact of the Abbasid rulers on Pakistani culture.
3. How were the boundaries of India and Pakistan decided during the partition of British India in 1947?
4. What is Sharia?

 Research Project

Find out more about the building projects of the Mughal rulers. Use the Internet or a library to identify the characteristics of architecture in the Mughal Empire. How did the Mughal style impact other periods of architecture in Pakistan?

Prime minister Nawaz Sharif waves to supporters during a rally in Lahore. Sharif is leader of the Pakistan Muslim League, which currently holds a majority of seats in the National Assembly. Other major political parties include the Pakistan People's Party, the Awami National Party, and Jamiat-e-Ulema-e-Islam.

Politics, Religion, and the Economy

In some ways, Pakistan's modern history has been a long experiment with different types of government. Its constitution has seen many changes, and has frequently been suspended. The country has seen the violent rise and fall of its political leaders, and has lived through long periods of military governments. In fact, the army has ruled the country for about half of the republic's history. This rule has been spread out over three major periods, each of which was preceded by a period of democracy.

Pakistan's first period of democracy lasted from 1947 to 1958. The governing and lawmaking body then was the Constituent Assembly, which originally used the 1935 Government of India Act as a temporary constitution. In 1956, the government presented the country's first constitution, which set up national and provincial governments and gave a great deal of power to the president. Under the constitution, the president could suspend any form of government in Pakistan at any time. The document also emphasized that Pakistan was an Islamic republic, governed by the principles of Islam.

The first period of military rule, from 1958 to 1969, came about because the democratic government found it more and more difficult to keep order. The succeeding rise and fall of many political leaders only made the country more unstable. The army was called in to enforce law and order. Eventually, it overthrew the democratic government.

The first military government, led by General Muhammad Ayub Khan, banned all political parties and suspended the constitution. However, the general tried to include some elements of democracy in his military rule. Local constituencies, or communities of voters of about 1,000 people, each elected a representative called a Basic Democrat. The Basic Democrats formed a significant part of the government, although Ayub Khan did not trust them as policymakers. To secure his power, he personally appointed politicians to the highest levels of government.

Uncertain about the safety of his position, Ayub Khan resigned in 1969. His successor, General Yahya Khan, maintained Pakistan's military rule, but he also announced that democratic elections would take place in 1970. That year, the second phase of attempted democracy began.

Words to Understand in This Chapter

bicameral—made up of two separate and distinct lawmaking bodies.
fasting—abstaining from food or drink, especially for religious reasons.
judicial—of a law court or judge.
monotheistic—characteristic of a religion that believes in only one supreme God.
pilgrimage—a journey to a sacred place for religious reasons.

Pakistan's flag was adopted in August 1947, when the country became independent. The color green, the crescent moon, and the five-pointed star are traditional symbols of Islam. The white crescent represents progress, while the star represents light and knowledge.

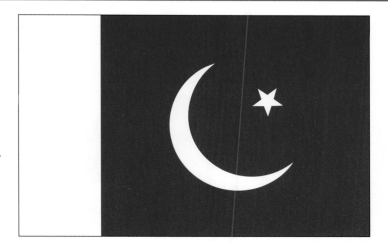

Zulfikar Ali Bhutto's government, which replaced Yahya Khan's, was not a military one, but neither was it a true democracy. The National Assembly, which by that point was Pakistan's legislative body, adopted a new constitution in 1973. Bhutto accepted the role of prime minister rather than administrator of martial law, though by the time of his arrest in 1977 he had effectively become a dictator.

After Bhutto's downfall, the constitution was suspended and martial rule was put into effect once again. This military phase lasted until 1988. The Provisional Constitutional Order of 1981 set out guidelines for a government under martial rule. A governing body was formed to supposedly act as a lawmaking body. In reality, General Muhammad Zia ul-Haq made all the laws.

In 1985, a new form of the constitution was adopted. This one was hardly democratic, giving almost all power to the president. One pivotal clause allowed the president to appoint any member of the National Assembly as prime minister. The president could also dismiss the prime minister at any time. During the 1990s, President Ghulam Ishaq Khan used this executive power to dismiss prime ministers Benazir Bhutto and Nawaz Sharif. When Sharif rose to power for the second time in 1997, he achieved changes in the constitution so that the president no longer had such power.

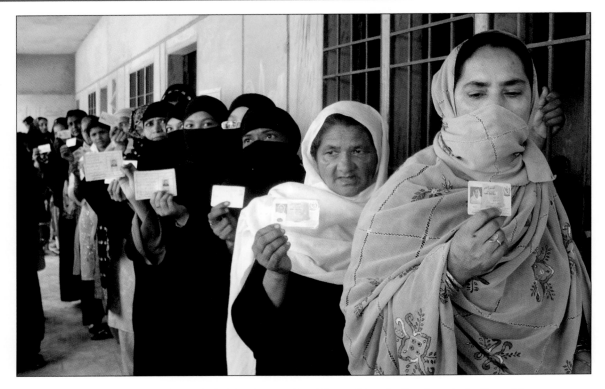

Pakistani women show their identity cards while waiting in line to vote in Karachi.

The constitution was suspended yet again in 1999, when General Pervez Musharraf returned the country to a third period of military rule. An altered constitution was restored in 2002.

During his administration, Musharraf served as both the president and head of the military, a consolidation of power that produced much controversy.

In 2010, President Zardari celebrated another revision of the constitution as a "historical moment." The 18th Amendment removed changes made during the military dictatorships of Zia-ul-Haq and Pervez Musharraf. The amendment makes it more difficult for military leaders to remove politicians and classifies suspending the constitution as treason. The revision also transferred certain powers from the president to the prime minister. For example the prime minister, with the approval of the National Assembly, now appoints military leaders and judges. These changes restored the spirit of the 1973 constitution, which framed Pakistan as a federal parliamentary democracy.

Pakistan has a ***bicameral*** parliament, made up of a National Assembly and a Senate. The National Assembly has 342 seats, 272 of which are directly elected by the people and are reserved for Muslim males. The constitution reserves 10 seats for non-Muslims and 60 seats for women. These representatives are chosen by the elected members of the assembly. Members of the National Assembly remain in office for five years.

The prime minister is elected from among the members of the National Assembly. Typically, the prime minister is the leader of the party that holds the most seats in the assembly. The prime minister then forms a government, choosing government ministers from among the remaining members. The National Assembly's main duties are to decide on government policy, including the budget, and to pass laws. Thanks to the 18th Amendment, greater power has passed from the president to the National Assembly.

Each of Pakistan's four provinces has its own lawmaking assembly, elected by the people. Although the provincial assemblies are vested with some authority, in Pakistan's rural and tribal areas it is still common for people to consult a tribal chief or the most powerful local landlord to resolve conflicts.

Provincial assemblies elect the members of the Senate. There are 104 senate members, most of whom keep their positions for six years. The Senate mostly acts as adviser to the National Assembly. Together, the National Assembly, the Senate, and the four provincial assemblies elect the president. Both the president and the prime minister must be Muslims.

The ***judicial*** branch of government is made up of the Supreme Court, the provincial high courts, and the district and session

A Pakistani policeman stands guard outside the Federal Shariat Court in Islamabad. Islamic laws were imposed in 1979; in recent years some human rights organizations and women's groups in Pakistan have tried to have the laws repealed, on the grounds that they discriminate against women.

courts. The district courts deal with civil cases, while the session courts deal with criminal cases. The Supreme Court is Pakistan's highest court, though when matters that pertain to Islam arise, a court of Islamic law known as the Federal Shariat Court will intervene.

Pakistan has many political parties. Some represent local or tribal interests and do not have much national influence. Two of the most important parties are the Pakistan People's Party and the Muslim League. The Pakistan People's Party, a secular organization, was founded on the ideals of socialism and modernization. Movement for Justice is the second-largest secular party. In addition to the Muslim League, Pakistan's religious parties include the United Action Front and the Islamic Assembly.

RELIGION

Islam, one of the world's great **monotheistic** religions, dominates Pakistan. Although the Pakistani government and most of its people are generally tolerant toward other religions, Islamic religion and civilization shape most aspects of life in the country.

The word *Islam* comes from the Arabic verb *aslama*, which means "to surrender" or "to submit." Surrendering to the will of God is the basis of Islam. According to traditional Islamic belief, the religion's founder, Muhammad (ca. 570–632), had his first vision of the angel Gabriel in 610. Accepting his calling as the messenger of God, Muhammad wrote down the messages that he received in visions. By the time of his death, he had recorded the long series of sayings that came to be known as the Qur'an. This holy book is supplemented by the Hadith—a collection of stories and sayings about Muhammad and his companions. When he established the new religion, Muhammad also founded a small community. It would become a great empire and spread the prophet's teachings throughout the Middle East and other parts of the world.

Like Jews and Christians, Muslims believe that there is only one God. In fact, Islam shares some of the basic beliefs of Jews and Christians, and Muslims consider Muhammad the last and greatest messenger in a long line of prophets that includes Abraham, Moses, and Jesus. Muslims believe in heaven and hell, and that there will be a Judgment Day. Muslims accept Jesus as an important prophet, but they do not believe he was the Son of God.

Every faithful Muslim follows five basic tenets of the religion called "pillars." The first is the *shahada*, or profession of faith, which every Muslim must recite, understand, and believe: "There is no God but Allah, and Muhammad is His prophet." The second pillar is *salat*, five daily prayers that are performed at certain times during the day. The prayers can be recited either individually or in a mosque. During these prayers, the believer faces in the direction of Mecca, where an ancient shrine to Allah known as the Kaaba is located. The third pillar is *zakat*, or the giving of alms. *Zakat*, which means "purification," is a kind of tax paid to the state to help the poor. The fourth pillar is *sawm*, or **fasting**. During the holy month of Ramadan, Muslims must abstain from eating, drinking, and certain other activities from sunrise until sunset. The fifth pillar is *hajj*, or **pilgrimage**. Muslims are expected to go to Mecca at least once in their lifetime to visit the Kaaba and perform special rituals, if they are physically and financially able to do so.

There are two main branches of Islam: Sunni and Shia. The split in Islam took place not very long after the death of Muhammad. Sunni Muslims believe that the first four imams, or religious leaders, who followed Muhammad were the prophet's true successors. Shiites, on the other hand, believe that only the fourth imam, Muhammad's son-in-law Ali, and his descendants, are rightful leaders. Today, the majority of Muslims in the world are Sunnis; they make up close to 90 percent of the total Muslim population, compared to 10 percent for Shiites (other minority sects make up the small remainder of followers). In Pakistan, Sunnis make up about 85 percent of the population, while the Shiites make up about 10 percent.

Two tiny sects of Islam also have followers in Pakistan. The Ismailis, or Aga Khanis, are a variant of Shia Islam. They believe that the Aga Khan, the head of the Nizari sect of Islam, is the only true Muslim leader. Another controversial sect is called the Ahmadiya. This group was founded in 1889 by Mirza Ghulam Ahmad, who claimed to be the new leader of Islam. Followers of Ahmadiya believe that it is the one true form of Islam, but most mainstream Muslims do not recognize the sect as legitimate. Most followers of Ahmadiya live in Pakistan, but there are also members in parts of India and Africa.

Some Muslims, both Sunnis and Shiites, practice a mystical form of the religion called Sufism. Sufis believe that they can draw closer to God through music, poetry, and ecstatic dances. Although today it is generally more common for Sufis to practice individually, some people still belong to groups known as orders. Holy men called *pirs* have many followers, and shrines built around the tombs of the pirs still attract people. Visitors gather at these shrines to pray, leave offerings, and celebrate festivals.

There are very small numbers of Christians, Hindus, and members of other religious groups in Pakistan. Together, they make up about 3 percent of the country's total population. Most Christians are converts from the lower castes of the Hindu system.

More than 10,000 Muslims can worship inside the prayer hall of the enormous Shah Faisal Mosque in Islamabad. This colossal structure attracts worshippers from across Pakistan and around the world. According to recent statistics, about 96 percent of Pakistan's population is Muslim.

Pakistan has a small Christian community, estimated at about 1 percent of the population.

The history of Christianity in the region goes back to the period of Mughal rule, when Jesuit missionaries and members of other Roman Catholic orders arrived in India to spread their faith. During the era when the British East India Company and the British Raj governed, Protestants worked to convert the inhabitants of the subcontinent.

Most Pakistani Hindus live in the Sindh province. Their religion is ancient and complex. Unlike most religions, Hinduism cannot be traced back to a single founder or religious leader. It developed over several thousand years, drawing from different cultures. Hindus accept the four Vedas, a collection of religious texts, as their sacred scripture. The writings include religious songs, prayers, descriptions of sacrifices, and instructions on how to meditate.

Hindus also believe in the caste system. Under this system, people are born into five different levels of society. Traditionally, they must associate and marry with people of the same caste. The Brahmans, or priestly caste, are at the top of the caste system. At the bottom are the so-called untouchables, who have the lowest social standing in Hindu society. Hindus also believe in many different gods—according to some sources, as many as 33 million. These gods are found in all aspects of life.

A small number of Pakistanis still follow an ancient religion called Zoroastrianism. The prophet Zoroaster founded the religion in Persia during the sixth century BCE. Zoroastrians believe in the supreme god Ahura Mazda, but they also believe in many other lesser gods. In Zoroastrian belief, history is a long struggle between good and evil, in which good will triumph. Zoroastrians are known for using fire in many of their ceremonies.

In the more isolated areas of Pakistan, ancient folk beliefs are still common. In the mountainous northern regions, many people believe in fairies and shamans. A

Pakistani Hindus hold earthen lamps to celebrate the festival of Diwali in their home in Peshawar.

shaman is a religious man who communicates between the world of humans and the world of the spirits by carrying out magical practices and rituals.

ECONOMY

During the thousands of years before Pakistan achieved statehood, the foundation of its economy was agriculture. Although the country's economy is still heavily dependent on agriculture, it has become more diverse.

Pakistan's working population is roughly 62 million strong. About 44 percent of the employed work in agriculture, but agricultural enterprises only contribute about 25 percent of the gross domestic product (GDP)—the total value of the goods and services produced by a country in one year. Some of the most important crops are wheat, rice, sugar cane, tobacco, fruits, vegetables, and the biggest agricultural export, cotton. Because much of the country is desert, or otherwise unsuitable for agriculture, massive irrigation projects have made farming possible in these areas.

About 20 percent of the workforce is employed in industry and manufacturing accounts for 21 percent of the GDP. When modern Pakistan became independent, it had only a few factories for industries such as sugar and cement production. Today, the country's manufacturers produce everything from cars to fertilizers.

However, power outages have slowed the economy and caused some factories to close. The power outages stem from an enduring energy shortage. Pakistan's energy infrastructure has not kept up with its growing population. The government has attempted improvements, but its proposal to build coal-based power plants failed due to environmental concerns. Prime Minister Sharif is now

Quick Facts: The Economy of Pakistan

Gross domestic product (GDP*): $884.2 billion (rank 27th in the world)
GDP per capita: $4,700 (rank 174th in the world)
GDP growth rate: 4.1% (rank 68th in the world)
Inflation: 8.6% (rank 168th in the world)
Unemployment Rate: 6.8% (rank 71st in the world)
Natural resources: land, extensive natural gas reserves, limited petroleum, poor quality coal, iron ore, copper, salt, limestone,
Agriculture (25.1% of GDP): cotton, wheat, rice, sugarcane, fruits, vegetables, milk, beef, mutton, eggs.
Industry (21.3% of GDP): textiles and apparel, food processing, pharmaceuticals, construction materials, paper products, fertilizer, shrimp.
Services (32.1% of GDP): government services, banking, insurance, transportation.
Foreign trade:
    Imports—$45.07 billion: petroleum, petroleum products, machinery, plastics, transportation equipment, edible oils, paper and paperboard, iron and steel, tea.
    Exports—$25.11 billion: textiles (garments, bed linen, cotton cloth, and yarn), rice, leather goods, sporting goods, chemicals, manufactures, carpets and rugs.
Currency exchange rate: 102.89 Pakistani rupees = U.S. $1 (2015)

*GDP, or gross domestic product, is the total value of goods and services produced in a country annually.
All figures are 2014 estimates unless otherwise noted.
Source: CIA World Factbook, 2015.

A merchant sells meat at the Raja Bazaar, the main shopping area in Rawalpindi.

pursuing plans for renewable energy plants using Liquefied Natural Gas. In the meantime, much of the country has limited electricity.

Textiles are Pakistan's most important export. Beautiful carpets are shipped all over the world, yet the carpet industry has been criticized because many of its goods are produced by child workers. Other major industries include industrial machines, processed food, and shipbuilding. Pakistan's mineral resources include coal, salt, and marble. The country also has some oil fields, as well as a large amount of natural gas.

About 33 percent of Pakistani workers are employed in service industries. These operations make up the highest-grossing sector,

An young Pakistani works at a brick kiln in Lahore. According to the International Labor Organization, more than half the world's quarter-billion child-laborers work in Asia, often under appalling conditions, facing sexual abuse and even slavery.

at 54 percent of the GDP. Services in Pakistan include banks, schools, hospitals, and transportation, all of which are owned by the state.

In its short modern history, Pakistan's economy has gone through periods of remarkable growth. The economy has also seen times of great insecurity, which has stemmed largely from the country's escalating national debt and high defense expenditure. Currently, about 28 percent of Pakistan's budget goes to military spending. According to many Pakistanis, one of the country's greatest problems is that enormous amounts of money are spent on the military, mainly for defense against India. The defense budget diverts money from areas such as health, transportation, and education. The government has also had mixed results in trying to bring in more revenue from taxes.

Although Pakistan faces many economic problems, there are reasons for optimism. The country has a highly skilled workforce; the level of poverty—especially extreme poverty—is going down; and new crops, fertilizers, and irrigation projects continue to improve Pakistan's agricultural potential. Many experts feel that if the country could overcome its debt and its reliance on military spending—both of which depend heavily on its relations with India—it could move to the forefront of developing nations.

 Text-Dependent Questions

1. What form of government did the constitutional reforms of 2010 reinstate?
2. Name the five pillars of Islam.
3. What is Pakistan's most important export?

 Research Project

Use the Internet or a library to explore Pakistan's child labor problem. Determine the factors that impact child labor rates and brainstorm strategies to improve the situation.

A Pakistani cook prepares Seekh Kabab, a traditional dish of the region, at a food-park in Islamabad. Seekh Kababs are elongated rolls of meat which are cooked on skewers over a charcoal fire. Pakistan has a rich variety of different kinds of foods.

The People

Pakistan is one of the world's great ethnic melting pots. Its people have come together from all the major ethnic groups of South Asia. Various factors have contributed to this diversity, including the conquering empires that have swept through the region as well as massive migrations and refugee movements. A visitor to Pakistan thus cannot assume that the people of one region will look, talk, and behave in the same way as other people of Pakistan. Although this diversity has caused much tension within the country, it is also the source of a wonderful variety of cultures and lifestyles.

PUNJABIS

Punjabis make up the largest ethnic group in Pakistan—about 45 percent of the population. They are primarily centered in the historic Punjab region. Since Pakistan's independence, they have dominated the country in the political arena and the military, which has become a source of resentment for some people of other ethnic groups. Critics of Punjabi power have even said that the country has effectively become "Punjabistan."

The traditional language of the Punjabis, also known as Punjabi, is more closely related to Urdu than any of Pakistan's other traditional languages. In recent years, more and more Punjabis have been exploring their language in areas such as literature and music. This investigation often includes the study of the several **dialects** of Punjabi, or its most popular variant, Siraiki, spoken by 10 percent of Pakistanis.

The Punjabis belong to a largely agricultural society. Most Punjabis today are farmers and craftsmen, as their ancestors have been for thousands of years. In some parts of the Punjab, the farmers own the land that they cultivate. In other areas, a deeply entrenched class system still exists, in which members of a powerful upper class, known as the feudals, own the land and control the distribution of its produce. Many Punjabi cities have only been built recently, but the villages that they encompass are very old, as is their system of governance. In many places the traditional leadership, composed of a body of five elders, is dying out.

PATHANS

The Pathans, also called Pakhtuns or Pashtuns, represent about 15 percent of Pakistan's total population. Composed of many large

Word to Understand in This Chapter

dialect—a form of a language spoken by a group of people or in a specific region.
nationalist—relating to a political group that wants to form a separate and independent country.
refugee—someone who has been forced to leave their home country, usually because of a war or political or religious reasons.

A group of Punjabis pose for photographers while attending an international Punjabi language conference in Lahore. Punjabis are the largest ethnic group in Pakistan, and make up nearly half of the country's population.

tribes, they make up one of the world's largest tribal groups. Tribes include the Khattaks, the Afridis, the Bangash, and the Shinwaris. Through history the Pathans have had a reputation as fearless warriors, owing greatly to their successful stands against the British, Russians, and others who invaded their territory.

The Pathans are mainly settled in Afghanistan and in Pakistan's Khyber Pakhtunkhwa province. Some also live in northern Balochistan. (Within Khyber Pakhtunkhwa and Balochistan, there are official tribal areas that are administered by the government of Pakistan.) Because they are present in more than one country, many Pathans identify more strongly with their fellow Pathans than with Pakistan as a whole. One Pathan leader, Wali Khan, has described Pakistan as "a crowd brought together by an accident of history." Since the founding of Pakistan, many Pathans have argued for the formation of a separate homeland, to be called Pakhtunistan or Pashtunkhwa. At times Pathan groups have resorted to violence, hoping to bring this about.

The Pathan way of life is very traditional and is founded on a code called *pushtunwali*, or the way of the Pathans. Within Khyber Pakhtunkhwa's tribal areas, the laws that make up *pushtunwali* have more weight than the official laws of Pakistan. The code is based on a strong sense of honor. It also lays great emphasis on hospitality, which must be shown to friends, strangers, and enemies. The rules governing revenge are less easy for most Westerners to understand or embrace. The Pathans believe that insults or injuries must be avenged, sometimes by death. This is especially true for insults directed at women.

In the settled areas of Khyber Pakhtunkhwa, most Pathan tribes are agricultural. A large number of them operate on the feudal system, with ruling chieftains controlling the land. In the tribal areas, people earn their living mainly by raising livestock such as goats and cattle. Each village has its own council of elders. The Pathans obtained important positions in government and the military during the years of British control. Today, they still share some of the leadership responsibilities in Pakistan.

BALOCH

The Baloch are the smallest ethnic group in Pakistan, making up just about 4 percent of the population. However, their tribal homeland of Balochistan is Pakistan's largest province by far. Like the Pathans, the Baloch are made up of many different tribes. They originally arrived about 1,000 years ago from Iran, where there are still Baloch living today. In the interior of Balochistan, the tribes are still traditionally nomadic. They keep large numbers of sheep and goats, and move around to find grazing lands for their flocks. On the coast, the Baloch are fishermen.

As a group that follows longstanding tribal traditions, the Baloch take an ambiguous stance on the Pakistani government. While they feel that they are underrepresented in the government's decisions, they also prefer to live by their own laws. Their code of conduct is similar to that of the Pathans, to whom they are racially and linguistically related. The code of the Baloch is known as *mayar*, or honor, which includes both the principles of hospitality and of revenge.

Perhaps even more than the Pathans, the Baloch have long felt that they should have their own homeland. A strong **nationalist** movement has existed in Balochistan for many years. One Balochi tribal chief commented, "I have been a Baloch for several centuries.

Members of the Baloch tribe, armed with heavy weapons, make their way towards their camp in Kahan, Balochistan. Many Baloch feel that they should have their own homeland, and in recent years they have waged an insurgency against the government of Pakistan.

I have been a Muslim for 1,400 years. I have been a Pakistani for just over fifty."

Pakistan annexed Balochistan in 1948 against the wishes of the Baloch, and the tribes have fought wars for independence in 1948, 1968, and 1973–77. In each case, the army of Pakistan ruthlessly crushed the resistance. In the early years of the 21st century, the Baloch nationalist movement reemerged, and by mid-2004 Baloch nationalists were regularly conducting rocket and mortar attacks against government targets in the province. A violent fight for Baloch independence has continued for over a decade, with nationalist groups attacking a military center and other government

 Quick Facts: The People of Pakistan

Population: 196,174,380 (rank 7th in world).
Ethnic groups: Punjabi, Pathan (Pakhtun), Sindhi, Muhajir, Balochi, other.
Religions: Muslim 96.4% (Sunni 85-90%, Shia 10-15%), other (includes Christian and Hindu) 3.6% (2010 est.).
Language: Punjabi 48%, Sindhi 12%, Siraiki (a Punjabi variant) 10%, Pashtu 8%, Urdu (official) 8%, Balochi 3%, Hindko 2%, Brahui 1%, English (official; lingua franca of Pakistani elite and most government ministries), Burushaski and other 8%.
Age structure:
  0–14 years: 33.3%
  15–24 years: 21.5%
  25–54 years: 35.7%
  55-64 years: 5.1%
  65 years and over: 4.3%
Population growth rate: 1.49% (rank 80th in world).
Birth rate: 23.19 births/1,000 population (rank 71st in world).
Death rate: 6.58 deaths/1,000 population (rank 146th in world).
Infant mortality rate: 57.48 deaths/1,000 live births (rank 25th in world).
Life expectancy at birth: 67.05 years (rank 168th in world).
Literacy: 54.7% (2011 est.).

All figures are 2014 estimates unless otherwise indicated.
Source: Adapted from CIA World Factbook, 2015.

buildings in Quetta, and killing senior government officials. Likewise, the Pakistani government is accused of using excessive force against the militants, and even sponsoring the assassination of a top Baloch leader in 2006.

Balochistan is a very sparsely populated area, and neither the present Pakistani government nor previous foreign governments have ever really succeeded in controlling the region. Although tribes have used this independence to preserve their traditional way of life and government, they are less modernized than other ethnic groups in Pakistan. There is little opportunity for formal education, and the Baloch have not benefited fully from the rich natural resources of their province.

SINDHIS

The Sindhis make up 14 percent of the total population of Pakistan. Their traditional language, Sindhi, is similar to Punjabi. Less than half of the residents of Sindh are Sindhis, and many continually feel threatened by the immigrant groups moving to the province, particularly to the large port city of Karachi. This has contributed to ethnic conflicts.

In many ways, the Sindhis resemble their neighbors in India more than most of Pakistan's other ethnic groups. Although Sindh was the first region of Pakistan to accept Islam, it is also home to more Hindus than any other part of the country. Even among the Muslims of Sindh, many Hindu traditions remain. For instance, the Sindhis greet each other in the Hindu manner, by pressing both hands together and bowing.

Sindh has often been regarded as the most explosive region of Pakistan. A Sindhi separatist movement existed even before the division of India and Pakistan, and it has lasted in defiance of the government's repression of Sindhi language and culture. Although urban Sindh is home to the country's most important financial and military institutions, there is a great deal of poverty in the small towns and villages of rural Sindh.

In the past, the Sindhis lived mainly by hunting. The Hindus of Sindh still hunt extensively today, though most residents of the province rely on agriculture to live. The feudal landlord system governs most of the province's agriculture. In southeastern Sindh, salt mining is a major source of income.

MUHAJIRS

The Muhajirs are markedly different from the other groups who make up the population of Pakistan. Strictly speaking, they are not an ethnic group. The word muhajir means **refugee** or "migrant." The Muhajirs include the Muslims who fled from India to Pakistan during partition, as well as their descendants. They belong to the different ethnic groups of India. Most Muhajirs speak Urdu, as well as the traditional languages of their ethnic groups. They often wear traditional Indian dress and follow Indian customs. Although there are Muhajirs all over Pakistan, most of them live in Sindh, especially the cities of Karachi and Hyderabad. About two thirds of the population of Karachi is Muhajir.

The position of the Muhajirs in Pakistani society has always been a difficult one. They suffered a great deal at the time of the partition, when hundreds of thousands of Muslim refugees were killed as they tried to flee India. The Muhajirs generally feel that they were the architects of Pakistan, and that the new nation could not have come about without their efforts. At first, they received many advantages in Pakistani society. Because they were generally well educated and fairly wealthy, the Muhajirs took over many of the best jobs in Sindh, as well as positions in the government. This stirred up resentment among the Sindhis.

During the 1960s, however, the Muhajirs began to lose the advantages they had once enjoyed. Political changes meant that important positions once occupied by Muhajirs were now given to members of other ethnic groups. Many Muhajirs began to demand equal status with Pakistan's other ethnicities, and a strong separatist movement emerged. Altaf Hussein, leader of the Muhajir Qaumi Movement (MQM), stated, "We would like the people of Pakistan to be one nationality, but how can that be when primary education books show four pictures of the nationalities of Pakistan—Punjabis, Pathans, Baloch and Sindhis? We are the ones who sacrificed our wealth and assets to come here, yet it seems we are not considered full Pakistanis." Some even say that their original status as refugees has not really changed.

Today, most Muhajirs still work in areas such as business and finance. They often live in large family groups, with many members of the extended family in the same house. Due to the challenges that they have faced, Muhajirs have become a tightly knit political community in spite of their varied backgrounds. Many of them continue to demand full recognition as an ethnic group.

FAMILY LIFE

Families are the foundation of Pakistani life. In the larger cities, families are gradually becoming more like Western families. A household may be made up of only the parents and the children, and perhaps a few other family members. However, members of extended families are still closely tied to each other, even if they may not live together.

Traditionally, many generations of one Pakistani family live together in the same house. The older members of the family have the greatest authority and must be shown more respect than anyone else in the family. Family members who are able to earn a living are responsible for looking after the children and those who can no longer work.

In Pakistan, marriages are usually arranged. It is uncommon for a young person to remain unmarried. Most married couples aim to have many children. Muslim parents believe that their greatest responsibility is to teach their children the beliefs and ways of Islam. In general, boys are valued more highly than girls. Sadly, because of widespread poverty, many Pakistani children start working at a very young age, especially in the carpet industry.

In general, the men and women of Pakistan have separate social lives. Men tend to socialize outside the home, in places such as teahouses and bazaars. The life of a Pakistani woman revolves around her children and her female friends. Some women stay in seclusion in keeping with the code of purdah. If they go outside, they are expected to wear a veil.

EDUCATION

Even at the primary level, Pakistani children are not required to go to school. Like so many other areas of Pakistani life, education has suffered because of the government's emphasis on military spending. Only about half of all adults can read and write. Pakistan's literacy rates are lower than those of many other South Asian countries.

Malala Yousafzai has become a hero to girls and women worldwide. She is an advocate for education and for greater opportunities for women in Muslim countries.

Some Pakistani schools are government-run, while others are private. The government schools emphasize Islamic teaching. Private schools, which are common in the larger cities, also include religion as a subject; however, they give more attention to academic subjects. While Urdu is the main language of instruction in government schools, private schools tend to use English.

Men and women can learn a trade

Pakistani schoolboys play outside a primary school in the village of Gah in the central Punjab province. Because education is not mandatory in Pakistan, fewer than half of all Pakistani adults can read or write.

at a specialized school or attend a university or college. Classes at the university level are taught in Urdu and English, and many Pakistanis study for degrees in areas such as engineering and agricultural science. However, as a result of corruption in the Pakistani educational system, the country's university degrees are often not highly regarded in other parts of the world.

ARTS, CULTURE, AND ENTERTAINMENT

Pakistan has a long tradition of religious poetry and music, some of which has been interpreted in new ways for a modern audience. Even today, most well-known Pakistani writers are poets. The most famous poet in Pakistan's history is Dr. Allama Muhammad

Iqbal, who was the first person to bring the idea of a separate Muslim state to a wide audience. Many of his poems deal with the struggle for freedom, especially for the poor and oppressed.

Another distinguished poet is Faiz Ahmed Faiz (1911–84), who in 1963 became the first Asian poet to win the Lenin Peace Prize. He was also nominated for the Nobel Prize. His poems deal with revolution and social justice, with love as the overriding theme.

Pakistan is famous for two forms of artistic expressions known as *qavvali* and *ghazal*, which combine poetry, music, and religion. *Qavvali* is devotional music, meant to bring the performers and the listeners closer to God. The music has a strong rhythm with a hand-clapping chorus. Traditionally, *qavvali* is performed at a saint's shrine, but today it can also be heard in nonreligious settings. Nusrat Fateh Ali Khan, the most famous performer of *qavvali*, wrote and performed with musicians from many different parts of the world. *Ghazal*, a related form, is love poetry that may also have a religious dimension. This form has also become very popular in Pakistani film music.

Rock and pop music have a major following among the young people of Pakistan. Musicians often combine elements of traditional Pakistani music with the guitars and heavy rhythm of rock music. Some popular Pakistani rock groups include Laal, Khumariyaan, and Noori. Laal promotes conversa-

A folk musician performs on a traditional stringed instrument of Pakistan.

tions about controversial topics, such as freedom of speech, feminism, and the military's role in politics. The band promotes social justice in Pakistan, using the Internet as their primary platform. Their activism led the Pakistani government to shut down access to the band's social media pages from within the country.

FOOD

Pakistan's food, like so many other products of the culture, combines aspects of India and of the Middle East. Although somewhat less spicy than Indian food, much Pakistani food is still hot by Western standards.

Bread and meat are the staples of the Pakistani diet. Bread is commonly called *roti*, but there are many different varieties. *Chapati* is a kind of flatbread served with all foods, while *paratha* is a thicker flatbread that is fried in oil and may have a vegetable filling. Most Pakistani dishes contain meat in some form. *Korma*, meat in a spicy yogurt sauce, is very popular, as are *tikka kebabs*, pieces of chicken, mutton, or seafood barbecued or baked on a skewer. A great many dishes are made with yogurt. There are many varieties of *raita*, a yogurt sauce made with salt, pepper, spices, and chili peppers. *Halva*, a sticky sweetmeat, is one of the most popular desserts.

Of course, recipes vary from region to region in Pakistan. In Pathan areas, the *chapli kebab* is a kind of burger made from mutton, shaped like the sole of a sandal. At a traditional Pathan meal, guests are served several chickens, as well as a goat or sheep.

POPULAR CELEBRATIONS AND FESTIVALS

Pakistan's main festivals are Muslim. The most important are Ramadan, a religious observance that lasts for an entire month, and various religious feasts. Unlike the Western calendar, the Muslim calendar is lunar, which means it is based on the cycles of the moon. Thus, the days of the two calendars do not completely align and Muslim festivals fall at a different time every year.

Ramadan takes place in the ninth month of the Muslim calendar. It is believed to be the month during which the prophet Muhammad received the first revelations from Allah. In observance of Ramadan, devout Muslims abstain from food or drink each day between sunrise and sunset. They spend much of the day praying and meditating on the principles of Islam. The evenings are a time for celebration. Friends and family visit each other, exchange gifts, and enjoy special meals after sunset.

At the end of Ramadan comes Eid al-Fitr (the Feast of Fast-Breaking), also called Chhoti Eid (Small Eid). Eid al-Fitr begins after the appearance of the new moon, which marks Shawwal, the

Pathan mountain men in rolled felt caps and woolen shawls shop for produce from the Punjab plains in the Peshawar bazaar.

month following Ramadan in the Muslim calendar. At the start of the festival, the men go to the mosque for special prayers. Throughout Eid al-Fitr, Pakistanis wear colorful traditional clothing and eat elaborate meals with their friends and family. Dancing, music, and gifts are all part of the celebration, as is the traditional sacrifice of a sheep. It is also customary for families to visit their relatives' graves.

The other great festival is Eid al-Adha, or Feast of the Sacrifice (also called Bari Eid, or the Big Eid). The celebrations for this festival are quite similar to those for Eid al-Fitr. They include prayer, feasting, and the giving of gifts. Eid al-Adha is celebrated for more than one reason. It recognizes the end of the period during which the *hajj*, or pilgrimage to Mecca, is performed. It also remembers an event described in the Qur'an in which the Patriarch Abraham demonstrated that he was willing to sacrifice his son to Allah. Just before Abraham committed the act, an angel of God intervened and provided him with a sheep to sacrifice instead. Muslim families who can afford it sacrifice a sheep, goat, camel, or cow. They share the meat with their friends, neighbors, and the poor. The meat is eaten for several days after the start of the Eid.

Another festival, Moulid an-Nabi, celebrates the birthday of Muhammad. This festival lasts only one day. Muslims say prayers and exchange sugary sweets, often in the shapes of animals and dolls.

Pakistan has some public non-religious holidays. Most of these have to do with political events in the country's modern history. Pakistan Day, on March 23, marks the day in 1956 when a resolution declared Pakistan an Islamic republic. Pakistan's Independence Day is August 14, when the country declared its independence in 1947. Another anniversary is September 11, marking the death of Mohammed Ali Jinnah. These holidays fall on the same day every year in the Western calendar.

Pakistan clubs participate in a cricket match at Jinnah Stadium in Sialkot.

SPORTS AND RECREATION

The people of Pakistan love all kinds of sports, and their country's teams have participated at the highest levels of world competition. Pakistan is known for its soccer players, but the country's favorite sports are probably cricket and polo. All over the country, wherever there is a flat piece of ground, both children and adults can be seen playing cricket. Pakistan's traditional cricket rival is India. Polo, a centuries-old game played on horseback, was revived by the British during their rule in the subcontinent. Pakistan is known for the aggressive style of its players and for having the world's highest polo grounds. They are located in Shandur Pass, sitting at an elevation of 12,140 feet (3,700 meters) in northern Pakistan.

Pakistan has some annual festivals centered around competitions. One of them is a kite-flying tournament called Basant, which takes place around the beginning of March. Celebrated all over the subcontinent, Basant is held in Pakistan in Lahore. In the competition, the strings of the large kites are coated with ground glass, which makes them sharp so that they can cut the strings of other kites. The objective is to cut as many of the opponents' kite strings as possible.

In the spring, Lahore is also the site of the Horse and Cattle Show, an agricultural fair. Participants show their livestock for prizes, race their horses and dogs, and perform traditional dances.

Text-Dependent Questions

1. Which group has a strong presence in politics and the military?
2. Describe the Pathan code of honor.
3. Describe the festival of Eid al-Fitr.

Research Project

Learn more about the history of the Baloch quest for an independent homeland. What arguments support Baloch independence? What factors have kept Balochistan a part of Pakistan?

Muslims walk into the Shah Faisal Mosque in Islamabad. The city was founded in the 1960s to be the capital of Pakistan; since 1990 the population has grown from about 250,000 to approximately 2 million.

Cities and Communities

The villages and cities of Pakistan illustrate the country's mixed character as young republic and ancient territory. While the capital, Islamabad, is only half a century old, Peshawar and other cities date back over 2,000 years. Because such a variety of landscapes, cultures, and historical events have shaped the country's communities, everyone's Pakistan is different. In spite of this diversity, these places also share a particularly Pakistani identity.

ISLAMABAD

Islamabad, the capital of Pakistan, is located in the north of the Punjab, on the Potwar Plateau, though it is not officially part of the province. Similar to the way the U.S. capital, Washington, is located in the District of Columbia (D.C.), Islamabad has its own district, the Islamabad Capital Territory.

Islamabad, which had a population near 2,000,000 in 2012, is not one of Pakistan's larger cities. It was recently established, in contrast to its twin city, Rawalpindi, which dates back over two centuries. At the time of Islamabad's construction in 1961, Karachi was the capital of Pakistan. However, it had been decided that Karachi, on the southern coast, was too remote to be the capital. Although Islamabad is now over 50 years old, it is still undergoing development.

Unlike most of Pakistan's cities, Islamabad is built on a very open and modern plan. It has parks, shopping centers, and wide streets, most of which run in straight lines. Islamabad is divided into zones, including the business district (or Blue Area), the diplomatic enclave, and the main educational and shopping areas. The shopping areas are composed of bazaars, or markets, selling food, clothing, toys, and many other things. The most famous of these is Juma Bazaar, which sells Pakistani and Afghan handicrafts on Sundays.

Islamabad's most distinctive attraction is the Shah Faisal Mosque, said to be the largest mosque in the world. The building's architecture is very modern; its minarets, or towers, remind many people of space rockets. Islamabad's governmental buildings, including the Presidential Palace, the Parliament Building, and the Supreme Court, also have dramatic structures with soaring walls and sharp edges. This district was the center of anti-government protests in 2014, which largely shut down the Sharif government for several months. Shakarparian Park is known for its jasmine and

Words to Understand in This Chapter

epic—relating to a story of a legendary hero or great adventure.
inlaid—set in the surface of a material to provide decoration.

rose gardens, and its views of both Islamabad and Rawalpindi. Outside the city, the Margalla Hills National Park is home to many wild animals.

Islamabad is mainly a government town, with many diplomatic operations. Islamabad's scientific institutes include the Atomic Research Institute and the National Health Center. Pakistan's military headquarters is close-by in Rawalpindi. Islamabad also has some manufacturing industries, as well as several farms producing dairy and vegetables.

LAHORE

The second-largest city in Pakistan, Lahore had a population of over 9 million in 2014. It is the capital of the Punjab province and is located in the eastern region, less than 20 miles (33 km) from the border with India.

Lahore is an ancient city, with origins steeped in Hindu mythology. Sources say that it was founded by Loh (or Lava), son of Rama. Rama is the hero of the great Hindu **epic** poem, *The Ramayana*. In 1036, Lahore became a Muslim possession when Turks conquered the city. In 1206, the sultan of Delhi, Qutb ud-Din, was crowned in Lahore and he became India's first Muslim ruler.

Over the next few centuries, several Muslim dynasties brought Lahore under their control. The city was often threatened by the Mongols, an Asian people whose conquests spread from modern-day China as far west as modern-day Germany. Lahore became one of the great cities of the Muslim world when the Mughal Empire took power and captured the city in 1524. Over the next 100 years, the Mughals raised great buildings, including palaces and temples. However, the city's decline had begun even before the Sikhs took control of it in 1767. The British were the next major power to capture the city, in 1846. After the creation of Pakistan in 1947, Lahore became the capital of the West Punjab province, later of West

In Lahore, Muslims pray inside a shrine at the tomb of Data Ganj Bakhsh, a Muslim teacher who practiced the mystical form of the religion known as Sufism. Data Ganj Bakhsh is considered the first major Sufi teacher to visit the subcontinent, and he wrote several books on Sufism, including Kashfu'l Mahjub, the first book on mysticism in the Persian language.

Pakistan, and finally of the Punjab province.

There are many layers of history underneath present-day Lahore. The city's main street is the Mall, or Shahrah-i-Quaid-i-Azam, which dates back to the British era. It is lined with the great buildings built by the British—everything from houses for guests of the state to the courthouses.

The Old City, in the northern part of Lahore, predates British rule. Near Lahore Fort, which was erected by the Mughals, there are several Sikh monuments. One of the most famous of these is the *samadhi* (cremation site) of Ranjit Singh, Lahore's greatest Sikh ruler. The Badshahi Mosque, located near the *samadhi*, was built by the Mughals in the 17th century. Its magnificent walls and towers of red sandstone seem to glow with their own light. This mosque is one of the largest in the world.

The Lahore Fort has been declared a UNESCO World Heritage Site. It contains palaces and other buildings built by several of the most important Mughal rulers. The Alamgiri Gate, on the west side of the fort, is so big that several elephants were able to parade through it at once. Elsewhere in the city, the Lahore Museum has one of the world's greatest collections of Indian artifacts. Just outside the city are other monuments such as Jahangir's Tomb, the grave of one of the great Mughal rulers. Its walls are **inlaid** with the 99 names for God listed in the Qur'an. Lahore is an important industrial center. Some of its major manufacturing industries include textiles, iron, and steel. Service industries, such as engineering and financial companies, are also growing in the city. Lahore is home to several educational institutions, including the University of the Punjab. Dating from 1882, the university is Pakistan's oldest school of higher education.

KARACHI

With a population of over 23 million in 2013, Karachi is the largest city in Pakistan. It lies on the southeastern coast of Pakistan, in the flat desert lands near the Indus River delta.

Karachi's history began quietly. It was originally a tiny community of fishers, one of whom was named Kalachi. It was then named Kalachi-jo-Kun, "the deep ditch of Kalachi." In 1795, one of the ruling Sindhi dynasties built the fort of Manora at Kalachi. In 1839, a British ship anchored off Manora and took the fort without a struggle. The British developed Karachi—as the town became known—into the capital of the Sindh province. It also became one of the most important British military centers and a port for the export of grain, cotton, and other products. The population grew rapidly, reaching 50,000 by 1848. For decades, the British continued to

A family takes a camel ride at dusk along Karachi's popular Clifton Beach. Karachi is the largest city in Pakistan, with a population of around 23 million.

pour money into Karachi, making it one of the world's greatest ports.

In 1947, the partition of British India sent millions of refugees into Pakistan. Many of these refugees went to Karachi, forcing the city to expand rapidly to accommodate them. The city was Pakistan's first capital until 1959, when the seat of government was moved to Rawalpindi, and then to Islamabad. Today, Karachi is still home to large numbers of refugees from Afghanistan and Bangladesh; people from economically disadvantaged areas of Pakistan also come to the city looking for work.

Karachi and its suburbs are spread out over an area of 560 square miles (1,450 sq km), from the coastline and swamplands into the desert. Its four major roads run from west to east, out from the Old City. One of these roads, Mohammed Ali Jinnah Road, is the site of the tomb of Pakistan's founder. To the east of the Old City, the Saddar Bazaar is Karachi's main shopping area. Closer toward the harbor are many other markets, selling everything from traditional carpets and pottery to books and maps. Unlike Islamabad, Karachi does not have many parks, but it does have several popular beaches.

Karachi's architecture reflects both old and new styles. There are buildings from the time of the British, modern high-rises, and palaces built in the styles of India's greatest empires. The Avari Renaissance Towers Hotel is the tallest building in the country.

Karachi is Pakistan's leading industrial center. Its factories produce automobiles, refined oil and petroleum products, ships, textiles, processed foods, and many other products. It is also a center for entertainment, scientific research, and the media.

PESHAWAR

Although its residents simply call it Shehr, or "the City," Peshawar's official name means "the Place at the Frontier." The city is located close to the border with Afghanistan, a country with which it has always been closely linked. Peshawar, with a 2014 population of over 2.5 million, is the capital of Khyber Pakhtunkhwa.

Many cultures meet in Peshawar. For hundreds of years, writers have described the city's atmosphere of mystery and danger. Travel writer Jonny Bealby called it "a storybook town, echoing the world of Harun-al-Raschid," in reference to the famous Arab ruler who appears in many of the wondrous tales of the *Thousand and One Arabian Nights*.

Peshawar dates back about 2,000 years, when it was called Pushapur ("the city of flowers"). It first achieved fame as one of the capitals of the Buddhist empire of the Kushans, who ruled during the first and second centuries CE. Traces of the ancient Buddhist civilization still remain. Peshawar has a Buddhist *stupa*, or shrine. At the height of the Kushan Empire in the second century, the shrine was a place of pilgrimage, but as the empire declined so did the city. Largely forgotten by the successive Indian empires, Peshawar was invaded by the Afghans, the Persians, and the Mongols over several centuries.

Peshawar did not regain its status as a major city until the 16th century, when the Mughal Empire rose to power in the Indian sub-continent. The Mughal emperor Babur named the city Begram and rebuilt its fort. It was his son, Akbar, who gave the city the name it bears today. Although nominally part of the Mughal Empire, Peshawar fell under Afghan control during the 18th century. In the early 19th century, Peshawar fell to the Sikhs, who lost it to the British in 1848. The British made the city their headquarters on the frontier. During the long Soviet-Afghan war (1979–89), it was a major center for Afghan *mujahideen* operations and refugee relief.

Peshawar is still a major stopping point on the Grand Trunk Road, which connects Kabul, Afghanistan, with Calcutta, India. Trains connect Peshawar to several of Pakistan's most important cities, including Lahore and Karachi. Modern Peshawar has two main sections: the Old City and the Cantonment, a relic of the colonial period.

The Old City is where visitors will find Peshawar's most fascinating buildings, as well as the many bazaars for which the city is famous. Along Qissa Khawani, or the Street of Storytellers, there were once many teashops where locals and visitors would exchange tales. Many of the teashops are no longer there, but it is still possible to buy Peshawar's famous brass and copper items, as well as clothing, spices, birds, and many other goods. Peshawar is one of the best places to buy beautiful and inexpensive carpets.

Bala Hisar Fort, which watches over the Old City, was originally built by Babur and rebuilt after the Sikh armies destroyed much of the district in the 19th century. Its enormous red stone walls dominate the Old City. Gor Khatri (Warrior's Grave) has been a sacred site for almost 2,000 years. Buddhists, Hindus, and Sikhs have all built shrines on the site. During the Mughal period, it was made into an area where rich merchants could stay the night and keep their goods safe. The white Mahabat Khan Mosque, built in 1630 by the Mughals, is another of the Old City's beautiful buildings.

Built for the British armed forces, the style of the Cantonment is very different from that of the Old City. Instead of the narrow, winding streets of the Old City, it has wide avenues and parks. The Cantonment contains buildings for government offices and British clubs, churches, living quarters for the British soldiers, and playing fields. The Peshawar Museum, which was once an assembly hall, has many artifacts from the different periods of the city's history, especially the Buddhist era.

About 10 miles (16 km) north of Peshawar, the narrow, steep-sided Khyber Pass runs from Jamrud Fort through the Sulaiman Mountains and across the border with Afghanistan. The pass has always been a strategically important area. The armies of many empires traveled through the Khyber Pass as they pushed their conquests eastward. The British fought several battles against the tribal peoples of the region.

Peshawar's major industries include sugar and food processing, steel, small firearms, furniture, and the manufacture of many traditional items such as carpets, sandals, turbans, and metalwork.

QUETTA

Quetta, the capital of the Balochistan province, is not a very big city. It had a population of about 1,000,000 in 2012. Its location is remote, high in the mountains near the border with Afghanistan, at the Bolan Pass. However, Quetta (which means "fort" in Pushtu, the primary language of Afghanistan) has been a strategically important defense post for a long time. Local people still call it by much older names: Shal, or Shalkot.

While records of Quetta go as far back as the 11th century, it had little significance on the world scene until the Mughals took the city in the 16th century. From 1730, the Khans of Kalat held the fort at Quetta, making it their northern capital. The Khans of Kalat were a powerful group of rulers in Balochistan whose power faced no outside threat for some time. In 1876, the British took over Quetta and made it into an important military town.

In 1935, tragedy struck when a major earthquake destroyed Quetta. At least 20,000 people died, and the city had to be rebuilt. Single-story houses later replaced the higher buildings that fell.

A Pakistani policeman watches commuters walk along a street in Quetta, the capital of the Balochistan province.

Quetta is home to the University of Balochistan, as well as a military staff college founded by the British. Because so many refugees from the Soviet-Afghan war live in Quetta, its bazaars are heavily stocked with Afghan goods. Generally, more Pathan than Baloch language is now spoken in and around Quetta. The Quetta Museum has artifacts from the nearby site of Mehrgarh. Beautiful attractions such as Hanna Lake, with its brilliant blue waters, and the oasis of Pir Ghaib have made Quetta a popular summer resort. In a relatively fertile area surrounded by mountains, it is a refreshing place to be during the extreme heat of the Balochistan summer. The nearby Hazarganji-Chiltan National Park is home to more than 200 varieties of plants, as well as leopards, snakes, and a type of wild goat known as the Chiltan markhor.

 ## Text-Dependent Questions

1. Which city has a strong Hindu background?
2. What is the largest city in Pakistan?
3. What location has been the route of multiple invasions of Pakistan from the west?

 ## Research Project

Make a list of Pakistan's capital cities throughout history, including those of the empires that preceded the country's independence. How did each location represent the ruling government and why did each change take place?

Because of its size and strategic importance in the region, Pakistan has forged relationships with the world's leading powers. (Top) U.S. president Barack Obama welcomes Prime Minister Nawaz Sharif to the Oval Office prior to their bilateral meeting in 2013. (Bottom) Sharif accompanies Chinese president Xi Jinping during his 2015 visit to Islamabad.

Foreign Relations

The history of Pakistan's foreign relations has been defined by the country's associations with its immediate neighbors—most notably, India—and Western superpowers such as the United States. Pakistan's relations with India have alternated between war and uneasy peace. Over the years the U.S. government has given much support to Pakistan, but it has also condemned its leaders for supporting Islamic *fundamentalists* and trading nuclear secrets with other countries.

For decades, Pakistan has been walking a diplomatic tightrope. Especially in recent years, the government has wavered between support for Islamic militants and expelling those groups from the country. Pakistan's uneasy mix of democracy and dictatorship has attracted criticism from Western governments. Because of its heavy dependence on foreign aid, Pakistan continues to seek good relations with the West while also maintaining ties with Muslim neighbors in Asia and the Middle East.

THE KASHMIR PROBLEM

The violence that accompanied the 1947 partition of British India, in which hundreds of thousands of Muslims and Hindus died, marked a poor start in Pakistan's relations with India. Kashmir became a source of conflict immediately after partition. As one of nearly 600 princely states ruled by a Hindu *maharaja*, Kashmir differed from the provinces of India, which the British government ruled directly. However, Kashmir's population, which was 85 percent Muslim, was difficult to pacify. The threat that the Muslim liberators imposed convinced the *maharaja* to accede to India in exchange for its military assistance. In 1948, the United Nations arranged a **cease-fire**, which has since been both broken and modified several times.

The wars that followed the first Indo-Pakistani War, which have led up to the present era, have claimed hundreds of thousands of lives. Since 1989 alone, it is estimated that at least 70,000 people have died in the ongoing Kashmir conflict. At least 8,000 people are missing. India has also claimed that Pakistan supports terrorist activity on its side of Kashmir and across the border into India. However, most Western governments avoid using the "terrorism" label to refer to Pakistan's activities in Kashmir. In general, the United States and China support Pakistan, while before its demise the Soviet Union sided with India.

 # Words to Understand in This Chapter

arsenal—a collection of weapons.
fundamentalists—strictly maintaining the core beliefs of a religion; today, often related to religious fanaticism.
cease-fire—a temporary agreement to stop fighting a war.

Over the years, the most frequently raised solution to the Kashmir problem has been to let the people of Kashmir themselves vote on the question of where they belong. So far, though, the Kashmiris have had little say in the fate of their own region.

Recent years have shown both hopeful signs and increased hostilities between Pakistan and India over Kashmir. A major cease-fire was reached in November 2003 and peace talks occurred in January 2004.

Complicating the peace efforts, however, have been recent attacks in India largely blamed on Pakistani militants. Many targets have been religious sites, including bombings in 2006 at a temple in the ancient pilgrimage city of Varanasi and an attack at a mosque in the southern city of Hyderabad in 2007. In July 2008, a series of explosions ripped through the western city of Ahmedabad in India, killing at least 45 people and wounding 160. Then in November 2008 ten Pakistani gunmen terrorized Mumbai, attacking hotels, cafés, a railway station, and a hospital. The attacks killed 166 people and injured hundreds more. The confirmation that these men were Pakistani citizens halted all peace negotiations and reinforced the notion that Islamic terrorists are to blame for all violence in India.

Finally in 2012, President Zardari and Indian Prime Minister Manmohan Singh broke the seven-year silence with high-level talks. However, little was accomplished. Prime Minister Nawaz Sharif has promised a new era of relations between the countries, but India refuses to engage in peace talks while Pakistani militants continue to break the cease-fire. In the fall of 2014, cross-border firing in Kashmir resulted in the deaths of at least 17 people, the worst violence in a decade.

INDIA AND THE NUCLEAR ARMS BUILDUP

The nuclear race in South Asia, in combination with the conflict over Kashmir, has also created enormous tensions between Pakistan and India. Aware that India was working to develop a nuclear program in the 1960s, Zulfikar Ali Bhutto declared that Pakistan should be ready to respond with equal force. In his book *The Myth of Independence* (1967), he wrote, "It will have to be assumed that a war waged against Pakistan is capable of becoming a total war. It would be dangerous to plan for less and our plans should therefore include nuclear deterrent." Shortly after India tested a nuclear warhead in 1974, Pakistan began a program to develop nuclear weapons under the direction of Abdul Qadeer Khan. By 1986, intelligence analysts believed the country had enough material to create a nuclear bomb, and in May 1998, Pakistan successfully conducted six tests of nuclear weapons in Balochistan. The tests came about two weeks after India had tested five of its nuclear weapons.

Since then, both countries have built up nuclear **arsenals**. In fact, as of 2014, Pakistan's stockpile was growing faster than the supply of any other country. India possesses about 100 nuclear weapons, while Pakistan's arsenal is estimated between 100 and 120 weapons. Therefore, a nuclear war between India and Pakistan would be devastating.

In 1990, during a time of great tension over Kashmir, the nuclear threat prompted U.S. president George H.W. Bush and Soviet premier Mikhail Gorbachev to issue a joint statement asking the two countries to carefully consider any military action. In 2001, after attacks by Muslim militants in Kashmir and India, both Pakistan and India moved troops to the Kashmir border, and the world feared that the two countries might be on the brink of nuclear war. The United States, Russia, China, and Great Britain sent diplomatic missions to defuse tensions in the region, and by the end of 2002 the danger had subsided.

The threat of nuclear war again made headlines during the

Kashmiri conflict of 2014, and casts a long shadow over the future of southwest Asia. Because the nuclear race and Kashmir are closely linked issues, nuclear tensions will almost certainly decrease if Pakistan and India resolve the Kashmir conflict. In addition to facing these ongoing dilemmas, Pakistan must also continually evaluate its place in the Muslim world, its views on fundamentalist organizations, and its relations with the United States.

THE UNITED STATES AND THE MIDDLE EAST

Pakistan emerged from a movement to create a Muslim state in South Asia, and since 1947 it has met some expectations as a leading Muslim country. However, the objectives of Pakistan's government, as well as the demands placed on it by other states, have sometimes pulled the country in a different direction. Pakistan's relations with the United States have been especially important in the development of its foreign policy.

Until the 1990s, U.S. views on Central and Southwest Asia—including countries such as Pakistan—tended to be shaped by the long-running Cold War and the uneasy relationship with the Soviet Union. In December 1979, when Russia invaded Afghanistan and Pakistan stepped in to help the Afghans, Pakistan began to figure importantly in the anti-Soviet interests of the United States. During the war in Afghanistan, Pakistan received a huge amount of foreign aid, especially from the United States. The *mujahideen*, the resistance fighters against the Soviets in Afghanistan, also received financial assistance. The United States, Pakistan, and other countries helped to recruit Muslims from countries around the world to fight along with the *mujahideen*.

After the fall of the Soviet Union and the waning of its influence in Central and Southwest Asia, Islamic fundamentalism grew in strength. In the 1990s, a fundamentalist group called the Taliban became increasingly powerful in Afghanistan, seizing power in

1996. The Taliban introduced an extremely rigid and harsh code of law. It also allowed al Qaeda, a terrorist group under the leadership of Osama bin Laden, to set up training camps for militants in its territory. Despite government opposition toward radical Islam in certain Central Asian countries, such as Tajikistan and Uzbekistan, interest in Islamic fundamentalism increased in Central Asia.

Pakistan had close ties with the Taliban, which was a Pathan-based group. Some of its members had studied in Pakistan with Jamiat-e-Ulema Islam (JUI), a fundamentalist political party. Many Pathans in the North-West Frontier Province, now Khyber Pakhtunkhwa, had long wanted to see a Pathan-based government in Afghanistan. But Pakistan's mostly Punjabi elite has long feared that Pathan nationalism in Afghanistan would attract the loyalty of Pathans in Pakistan and thus threaten the territorial integrity of the Pakistani state. Such fears nearly led to war between Afghanistan and Pakistan in 1954. The Pakistani military and intelligence leadership thus supported religious-based rather than ethnic Pathan-based leadership in Afghanistan. Indeed, the Pakistani intelligence service, called the InterService Intelligence (ISI), was instrumental in creating the Taliban in Afghanistan. Pakistani leaders also saw Afghanistan as Pakistan's defense-in-depth against India, its main strategic threat. That helps explain why Pakistan sent Kashmiri fighters to Taliban training camps.

U.S. leaders rarely paid attention to Pakistan's view of Afghanistan, or understood much about the complex historical legacy of the Pathan region that stretched across the Afghan-Pakistan border. But U.S. attitudes changed when it became clear that the Taliban was threatening Western interests with terrorist activity. The Taliban also became a target because of its oppressive treatment of women. By 1998, the United States had stepped up its attempts to capture or kill Osama bin Laden. That year bin Laden had engineered the bombing of the U.S. embassies in Kenya and

Tanzania through al Qaeda. As Pakistan continued to support the Taliban, U.S.-Pakistan relations became strained. Nawaz Sharif, the prime minister at the time, offered to help the United States track down bin Laden, but the plan did not survive the coup that overthrew Sharif and brought General Musharraf to power.

After the September 2001 terrorist attacks on targets in the United States, things changed quickly and dramatically. Osama bin Laden and al Qaeda were immediately singled out as responsible for the attacks. Pakistan quickly decided to support the United States, or at least to promise as much in public. Since the fall of the Afghan Taliban in December 2001, Pakistani troops have searched the northern regions of the country for possible terrorist hideouts among the tribal groups. In return, the United States has helped build Pakistan's infrastructure, and also helped train thousands of Pakistani teachers and doctors.

From 2009 to 2014, the U.S. provided about $6 billion in civilian assistance and disaster relief to the government of Pakistan. This aid went toward health care, education, clean drinking water, and flood relief.

Many Pakistanis are incensed about the U.S. military's Predator drone strikes against suspected terrorist targets in northwestern Pakistan. Prime Minister Nawaz Sharif has demanded an end to the strikes, calling them illegal and inhumane. Between 2004 and 2014, it is estimated that more than 2,000 people have been killed by drone strikes, including several hundred Pakistani civilians who were accidental casualties of the U.S. war on terror.

Militant groups within Pakistan have strongly criticized Pakistan's support for the United States, although a majority of Pakistanis approve of the policy.

Relations with the United States have influenced peace talks between Pakistan and India over the Kashmir situation. However, the discovery that Pakistani scientists sold nuclear secrets to other governments strained the relationship in the early 2000s and led the U.S. to reconsider some aid programs.

The relationship has remained rocky and unstable. Pakistani outrage against the U.S. erupted in June 2008 when a U.S. airstrike on the Afghan-Pakistan border killed 11 members of the paramilitary Frontier Corps. The target was a village that was home to al Qaeda militants. Anger again flared in 2011 following the killing of Osama bin Laden by U.S. troops on Pakistan soil and a NATO airstrike that accidentally killed 24 Pakistani soldiers near the Afghan border.

What remains to be seen is how relations between Pakistan and the United States will play out in a new era of democratic rule. Both Musharraf and Zardari were important allies of the United States in the "war on terror." Yet Nawaz Sharif was elected prime minister on an economic, not a security platform. Western leaders have become frustrated with his inconsistent, and sometimes soft, stance on Islamic militants. However, Sharif has met with high-level Western officials, including President Barack Obama, and he recognizes that Pakistan's economic struggles have a strong security component, especially when it comes to the lack of international investment.

The United States will continue to urge Pakistan's government to tackle extremely important and difficult tasks—notably, rooting out members of Islamist groups that want to topple Pakistan's government. In September 2014, the country experienced one of the worst terrorist attacks in its history when the Pakistani Taliban invaded a school in Peshawar. The militants killed nearly 150 people, mostly children. Sharif's government will need to suppress the Pakistani Taliban, the Afghan Taliban which continues to operate out of western Pakistan, and other militant groups if the prime minister wishes to significantly improve the Pakistani people's quality of life.

As it now appears, the policies followed by the Pakistani military and intelligence leadership toward Afghanistan have badly backfired. Rather than use radical religious militants in Afghanistan to control Pathan nationalism, the resurgent Afghan Taliban has stirred up Pathan religious militancy inside Pakistan. Radical Islamists took control of the Swat Valley north of Islamabad in the spring of 2009 and pushed to within 60 miles of Islamabad. This raised fears that the Pakistani state was in danger of collapse, and that Pakistan's nuclear weapons might end up in the hands of radical Islamists in league with al Qaeda. As long as Islamic extremists terrorize the country, the stability of Pakistan, the region, and the safety of the world will be in question.

 ## Text-Dependent Questions

1. What region is at the center of the Pakistani-Indian conflict?
2. Describe the influence of western powers, such as the United States, on the government of Pakistan.
3. What prompted Pakistan to develop nuclear weapons?

 ## Research Project

Use the Internet to find articles written by Pakistanis about the United States or other western countries. How do Pakistanis view Westerners and Western governments? What actions of the United States have supported or contradicted these views?

6500 BCE	Mehrgarh, one of the oldest recorded farming settlements, is established in the Balochistan desert.
ca. 2700	Significant settlements are made at Harappa and Mohenjodaro along the Indus; trade takes place between the two towns.
ca. 1500	The Aryans arrive in the Pakistan region; religious epics attributed to them eventually become part of the central scriptures of Hinduism.
ca. 530	Persian kings make the Pakistan region one of their provinces.
326	Alexander the Great takes the Pakistan region; retreats the following the year.
305	The Mauryan empire takes control of the Indus Valley and becomes the first great Indian empire.
60 CE	The Kushan dynasty conquers the northern Pakistan region and establishes its capital at Peshawar; Buddhism begins to spread across the Indian subcontinent.
ca. 570	Muhammad, founder of Islam, is born in Mecca in the Arabian Peninsula.
711	The Muslim general Muhammad bin Qasim invades Sindh.
750–962	The Muslim Abbasid dynasty appoints governors to rule over Sindh; major cultural exchange takes place between Muslims and Hindus.
1211	The Delhi Sultanate begins its rule over the subcontinent.
1526	Babur establishes the Mughal Empire.
1757	With the victory of the British army at the Battle of Plassey, the British East India Company becomes dominant in the subcontinent.
1799	Sikh emperor Ranjit Singh conquers Lahore.
1843	The British take full control of Sindh.
1845–46	The First Sikh War takes place between the British and the Sikhs of the Punjab; the British grant control of Kashmir to a Hindu ruler.
1849	The Second Sikh War ends with the Sikhs' defeat.
1857	The Indian Mutiny results in the end of the Mughal Empire and the start of the British Raj.
1885	The Indian National Congress is founded.
1906	The All-India Muslim League is founded.
1930	Dr. Allama Muhammad Iqbal suggests the formation of a separate Muslim state.

CHRONOLOGY

1940   Mohammed Ali Jinnah presents the Lahore Resolution for the creation of Pakistan.

1947   The partition of India and Pakistan takes place on August 14; in October, the first Kashmir War begins and lasts through 1948.

1956   Pakistan ratifies its first constitution, which declares the country an Islamic republic.

1958   General Muhammad Ayub Khan seizes power.

1965   The Second Kashmir War takes place.

1971   Civil war in East Pakistan ends in the creation of the independent country of Bangladesh.

1973   Zulfikar Ali Bhutto becomes prime minister of Pakistan.

1977   General Muhammad Zia ul-Haq imposes martial law.

1979   Bhutto is executed; after the Soviets invade Afghanistan, Pakistan becomes an Afghan ally in the ensuing war.

1988   Zia dies in a plane crash; Benazir Bhutto becomes the new prime minister.

1989   Islamic militants start a campaign to reclaim Kashmir.

1990   Bhutto is relieved of office and Nawaz Sharif becomes the new prime minister.

1998   India tests nuclear weapons; Pakistan holds its own tests two weeks later.

1999   Kargil conflict breaks out over area in Kashmir; General Pervez Musharraf imposes military rule.

2001   Following bombings in Indian Kashmir and Delhi, India and Pakistan prepare for war and station troops along Kashmir's Line of Control for a year.

2003   In December, a cease-fire is declared between India and Pakistan over Kashmir.

2004   The leaders of Pakistan and India discuss prospects for resolving the Kashmir problem and other issues that have divided their countries.

2006   President Musharraf signs a controversial peace agreement with seven militant groups, who call themselves the "Pakistan Taliban."

2007   In July, 102 people are killed during a military operation to crush a Taliban-style movement at a mosque in Islamabad; in November Musharraf declares a state of emergency, suspends Pakistan's constitution, and fires Chief Justice Iftakar Mohammed Chaudhry and the other judges on the Supreme Court; Benazir Bhutto is assassinated in December during a political rally.

2008   In June a U.S. airstrike on the Afghan-Pakistani border kills 11 members of the paramilitary Frontier Corps; in August Musharraf resigns. Asif Ali Zardari of the Pakistan People's Party is elected president; in September a truck bomb explodes outside the Marriott Hotel in Islamabad, killing 53 people.

2009   The United States offers $1 billion in aid to Pakistan, with the condition that the government take stronger steps against militants, al Qaeda, and Taliban forces.

2009   In August a U.S. drone attack kills the leader of the Pakistan Taliban, Baitullah Mehsud and a suicide bombing kills 120 people in Peshawar

2010   In April Parliament approves a major revision of the constitution; extreme flooding kills at least 1,600 people and affects more than 20 million Pakistanis.

2011   In March the prime ministers of Pakistan and India watch a cricket match together. U.S. Special Forces kill Osama bin Laden in Abbottabad; a NATO strike kills 24 Pakistani soldiers.

2012   Taliban gunmen attack 14-year-old Malala Yousafzai, an advocate for girls' education; a Taliban suicide bomber kills more than 20 people at a Shia Muslim procession in Rawalpindi.

2013   General Pervez Musharraf is arrested for dismissing the Supreme Court during his rule; the Taliban attack campaign events and voters during the parliamentary election; the Muslim League wins a majority in Parliament and Nawaz Sharif is elected to a third term as prime minister; Parliament votes for Mamnoon Hussain as president.

2014   Government officials hold peace talks with the Pakistani Taliban, but negotiations collapse after militants attack the Karachi airport. Anti-government protesters conduct a two-month sit-in in Islamabad with the unrealized goal of forcing Prime Minister Sharif to resign. Taliban fighters kill nearly 150 people at a Peshawar school.

2015   Taliban militants attack Shia mosques in Sindh and Peshawar and Christian churches in Lahore. In April gunmen kill a female human rights activist in Karachi.

SERIES GLOSSARY

autonomy—the right of self-government.

BCE and CE—an alternative to the traditional Western designation of calendar eras, which used the birth of Jesus as a dividing line. BCE stands for "Before the Common Era," and is equivalent to BC ("Before Christ"). Dates labeled CE, or "Common Era," are equivalent to Anno Domini (AD, or "the Year of Our Lord").

caliphate—an Islamic theocratic state, in which the ruler, or caliph, has authority over both the spiritual and temporal lives of his subjects and all people must obey Islamic laws.

civil society—the sum total of institutions, organizations, and groups promoting social and civic causes in a country (for example, human rights groups, labor unions, arts foundations) that are not funded or controlled by the government or business interests.

colonialism—control or domination by one country over an area or people outside its boundaries; the policy of colonizing foreign lands.

ideology—a system of beliefs, values, and ideas forming the basis of a social, economic, or political philosophy.

Islamist—a Muslim who advocates the reformation of society and government in accordance with Islamic laws and principles.

jihadism—adherence to the idea that Muslims should carry out a war against un-Islamic groups and ideas, especially Westerners and Western liberal culture.

nationalism—the belief that shared ethnicity, language, and history should form the basis for political organization; the desire of people with a common culture to have their own state.

Pan-Arabism—a movement seeking to unite all Arab peoples into a single state.

self-determination—determination by a people of their own future political status.

Sharia—Islamic law, based on the Qur'an and other Islamic writings and traditions. The Sharia sets forth the moral goals of an Islamic society, and governs a Muslim's religious political, social, and private life.

Shia—the smaller of Islam's two major branches, whose rift with the larger Sunni branch originated in seventh-century disputes over who should succeed the prophet Muhammad as leader of the Muslim community.

Sunni—a Muslim who belongs to the largest branch of Islam.

Wahhabism—a highly conservative form of Sunni Islam practiced in Saudi Arabia.

Zionism—the movement to establish a Jewish state in Palestine; support for the State of Israel.

FURTHER READING

Ali, Tariq. *The Duel: Pakistan on the Flight Path of American Power*. New York: Scribner, 2008.

Hussain, Zahid. *Frontline Pakistan: The Struggle with Militant Islam*. New York: Columbia University Press, 2007.

Khan, Yasmine. *The Great Partition: The Making of India and Pakistan*. New Haven, Conn.: Yale University Press, 2008.

Mansfield, Peter. *A History of the Middle East*. 4th ed. revised and updated by Nicholas Pelham. New York: Penguin Books, 2013.

Marsico, Katie. *The Assassination of Osama Bin Laden*. New York: Marshal Cavendish Benchmark, 2013.

Nazaw, Shuja. *Crossed Swords: Pakistan, Its Army, and the Wars Within*. New York: Oxford University Press, 2008.

Rashid, Ahmed. *Descent in Chaos: the U.S. and the disaster in Pakistan, Afghanistan, and Central Asia*. New York: Viking, 2008.

Schwedler, Jillian. *Understanding the Contemporary Middle East*. Boulder, Colo.: Lynne Rienner Publishers, 2013.

Sheehan, Sean, et al. *Pakistan*. New York: Cavendish Square Publishing, 2015.

Yousafzai, Malala, and Patricia McCormick. *I Am Malala: How One Girl Stood Up for Education and Changed the World*. Boston: Little, Brown Books for Young Readers, 2014.

INTERNET RESOURCES

http://www.state.gov/r/pa/ei/bgn/3453.htm

The U.S. State Department website has a thorough section on the background of Pakistan, including its economics, politics, and other information.

https://www.cia.gov/library/publications/the-world-factbook/geos/pk.html

The CIA World Factbook website provides a great deal of statistical information about Pakistan and its people. It is regularly updated.

www.mideasti.org

An extensive resource geared to educate Americans about the Middle East. This academic site includes loads of information for research.

www.un.org/english

The English-language web page for the United Nations can be searched for Pakistan-related stories and information.

www.bbc.com/news

The official website of BBC News provides articles and videos on important international news and events related to the Middle East and elsewhere.

www.aljazeera.com

The English-language website of the Middle Eastern news service Al Jazeera provides articles and videos on breaking news, as well as feature stories that provide background material, including profiles of leaders and essays reacting to major events.

www.fpri.org

The website of the Foreign Policy Research Institute includes informative essays by FPRI scholars on events in the Middle East.

INDEX

Numbers in *bold italic* refer to captions.

INDEX

PICTURE CREDITS

CONTRIBUTORS

Senior Consultant CAMILLE PECASTAING, PH.D., is acting director of the Middle East Studies Program at the Paul H. Nitze School of Advanced International Studies at Johns Hopkins University. A student of behavioral sciences and historical sociology, Dr. Pecastaing's research focuses on the cognitive and emotive foundations of xenophobic political cultures and ethnoreligious violence, using the Muslim world and its European and Asian peripheries as a case study. He has written on political Islam, Islamist terrorism, social change, and globalization. Pecastaing's essays have appeared in many journals, including *World Affairs* and *Policy Review*. He is the author of *Jihad in the Arabian Sea* (Hoover Institution Press, 2011).

The FOREIGN POLICY RESEARCH INSTITUTE (FPRI) provided editorial guidance for this series. FPRI is one of the nation's oldest "think tanks." The Institute's Middle East Program focuses on Gulf security, monitors the Arab-Israeli peace process, and sponsors an annual conference for teachers on the Middle East, plus periodic briefings on key developments in the region.

Among FPRI's trustees are a former Undersecretary of Defense, a former Secretary of the Navy, a former Assistant Secretary of State, a foundation president, and numerous active or retired corporate CEOs, lawyers, and civic leaders. Scholars affiliated with FPRI include a Pulitzer Prize–winning historian; a former president of Swarthmore College; a Bancroft Prize–winning historian; and a former Ambassador and senior staff member of the National Security Council. And FPRI counts among its extended network of scholars—especially its Inter-University Study Groups—representatives of many diverse disciplines, including political science, history, economics, law, management, religion, sociology, and psychology.

CLARISSA AYKROYD is a graduate of the University of Victoria in British Columbia, Canada. She has written and published fiction, reviews and criticism, travel writing, and educational writing for software programs. Her previous nonfiction works for children include books on the exploration of California, Native American horsemanship, and the history of Mexican government. Her interests include history, travel, music, Arthurian legend, and Sherlock Holmes.